St Petersburg across the River Neva

VIKING

IMPERIAL SPLENDOUR

Palaces and Monasteries of Old Russia

Prince George Galitzine

Photography
Earl Beesley and Garry Gibbons

VIKING

VIKING

Published by the Penguin Group
Penguin Books Ltd, 27 Wrights Lane,
London W8 5TZ, England
Viking Penguin, a division of Penguin Books USA Inc.
375 Hudson Street, New York 10014, USA
Penguin Books Australia Ltd, Ringwood,
Victoria, Australia
Penguin Books Canada Ltd, 2801 John Street,
Markham, Ontario, Canada L3R 1B4
Penguin Books (NZJ Ltd, 182–190 Wairau Road,
Auckland 10, New Zealand

Penguin Books Ltd, Registered Offices:
Harmondsworth, Middlesex, England

First published 1991
1 3 5 7 9 10 8 6 4 2

Photographs copyright ©Beesley Gibbons, 1991
Text copyright © Prince George Galitzine, 1991
The moral rights of the author and photographers
have been asserted.

A CIP catalogue record is available
from the British Library

ISBN 0-670-83558-7 UK edition
0-670-84143-9 USA edition

Frontispiece:
The Catherine Palace, Pushkin

Overleaf:
Church of the Virgin of Katsan, Kolomenskoe

Dedication page:
Sunrise over Novgorod

Colour separations
by Colorlito Rigogliosi s.r.l. Italy
Printed and bound in Italy
by Amilcare Pizzi SpA
Illustrations by Julie Wigg
Designed and Photographed by Beesley Gibbons Ltd

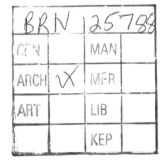

Contents

Introduction

Russia is such a vast country that one must be forgiven for having to generalize using the broadest of brush-strokes. This book does not attempt to offer a comprehensive portrait either of the history of Russian architecture or of the more familiar sights of Moscow and St Petersburg – there are plenty of books which cover those aspects very adequately. It is primarily a book of pictures, and as such the essential requirement is that they should be beautiful. One invariable ingredient ensures this – the breathtaking loveliness of the Russian landscape – and within our necessarily wide overview we take the reader through three general picture categories, corresponding roughly to three periods in Russian history.

From the first period, the pre-Muscovite, little remains for photography; it was a period of building in timber, and regular and frequent fires left nothing to posterity except some citadels – known in Russia as Kremlins – and ecclesiastical buildings in the form of churches and monasteries. This period stretches from the very beginning of Varangian (Viking) rule in the ninth century to the late fifteenth, and is known in the history books as the Kievan age. It is the age of the independent city-states of Novgorod and Pskov, of the capitals of the apanage principalities of Vladimir and Suzdal, which succeeded Kiev. This period also covers the two and a half centuries of the Tartar-Mongol occupation, and the beginning of Moscow's emergence as the dominant principality heading the struggle for liberation from the suzerainty of the Great Khan of the Golden Horde.

The second period broadly spans the sixteenth and seventeenth centuries. It covers the shaping of the Russian state, with the ascendancy of Muscovy and the strengthening of despotic power in the hands of the Tsar in Moscow; the reigns of Ivan III and his descendants, particularly the fifty-year reign of Ivan the Terrible; the Time of Troubles in the first years of the seventeenth century; and the establishment of the Romanov dynasty by its first three rulers.

The final period dates from the foundation by Peter the Great of the new capital of St Petersburg, and its growth and expansion by his successors, particularly his daughter Elizabeth, and by Catherine the Great. During this period secular building, starting with the Petrine epoch, flourished in the whole country, and particularly in and around both capitals – Moscow, the traditional one, and St Petersburg itself, with Baroque and Classical palaces for the nobility and their Imperial masters competing with European contemporaries in exuberance.

Throughout these periods the Russian Orthodox Church was active in every cultural sphere. Surprisingly, it so happened that the Tartars did not interfere in the religious life of the Russian people. The Church was even favoured by them, and obtained many privileges. Monasteries were exempt from having to pay the tribute they demanded elsewhere, and therefore flourished. The role of the Church in the arts and education, particularly of the young, was unique and more or less exclusive. Both Novgorod and Pskov had escaped the Tartar-Mongol invasion, and the result was that they each evolved their own character in the arts of building and ikon painting. In the same way, but later, Moscow also developed its own distinctive school of art. Predominant among the cultural heritage of the Orthodox Church are their numerous buildings, which provide many of the more spectacular sights in both city and countryside to this day. In Novgorod and Suzdal the authorities have set up open-air museums of architecture, bringing wooden churches and some representative secular buildings from remoter villages into one enclave for tourists and students to view. Although some of these timber churches date from the early eighteenth century, their designs are almost dateless and are highly original and creative. An interesting feature is the use in northern Russia of wooden shingles on the cupolas or onion-shaped domes. These are skilfully hewn freehand with an axe from aspen wood, and when weathered the aspen gives a silvery sheen when wet, which is most picturesque.

With the eighteenth century came the age of vast changes and expansion in the reign of Peter the Great – called the 'Giant Wonderworker' by Russia's favourite poet, Pushkin. It is interesting to note that many of his innovations and ideas, particularly in Westernization, had been initiated by contemporaries of his predecessors. His half-sister's Chief Minister and lover, Prince Vassily Galitzine (Golitsyn), first mooted the notion of emancipation of the serfs at the end of the seventeenth century, although it was not the subject of Imperial decree until 1861, a good five generations of monarchs later.

In this new climate it became the fashion among the richer and more enlightened families of the nobility to have their children taught by foreign tutors and governesses, and for the boys to be sent abroad to Europe, from where they brought home new ideas. Peter was the first Tsar to go to Europe, but the Empress Anna, his niece, was summoned from the West to occupy her throne, and Catherine the Great was a German princess who came to Russia to marry the heir to the Empress Elizabeth. The landed gentry very rapidly had to build or adapt their country houses to the new requirements dictated by fashion. Only the very rich and prominent nobles, such as the Dolgorukys, Galitzines and Sheremetievs, had houses built of masonry or stone. Old houses were mostly built of pine logs, and although very few of these have survived, we have drawings from artists such as Meyerberg, who describes houses and timber churches of the 1660s.

On the whole, masonry houses were not popular. Besides being more expensive to build, inadequate heating arrangements meant that they were much colder and damper than those built of solid pine blocks. Fire not infrequently reduced the main house, as well as its neighbouring buildings and outhouses, to a heap of ashes, and a new complex had to be built from scratch. Many of the architects who designed and supervised the building of these houses were self-taught, talented serfs belonging to the landlord. They sometimes designed churches too, and their work compared very favourably with that of architects of established reputation who had come from the capital especially for the job in hand, or had even been imported from abroad. In some cases these basically amateur architects had limitless resources of manual labour on which to call, because of the number of serfs available. Contrary to popular belief, the country houses outside Moscow were not lavish or architecturally monumental, and those near provincial capitals were even more modest and simple. Their main interest is historical or sociological. There are notable exceptions, however, and it is worth examining what most of them had in common, in order to give an idea of what sort of life they represented in their age.

Peter the Great's associate, Field-Marshal Count Boris Sheremetiev, bought a wooden house in a village called Kuskovo, a place known as a good hunting site which had been popular with Tsar Alexis, Peter's father. Kuskovo was then a few miles outside Moscow, but is now, of course, incorporated in Moscow's expanded township. Count Boris died in 1719, only four years after acquiring the property, and his six-year-old son, Peter, inherited. When he was thirty years old Peter Sheremetiev married Varvara (Barbara), the sole heir of the immensely wealthy chancellor, Prince Alexis Cherkassky, and this gave him almost unlimited means with which to convert the house into an exemplary summer residence.

The redesigned house was once again made of wood but on a stone pediment, in front of an artificially dug lake, with a white-pillared portico and a smart frontage and entrances through a surrounding fence. It is said locally that the lake was dug in twenty-four hours, to provide work for the locals during the famine and plague of the 1770s. The purpose of the house was to provide a venue for lavish balls and receptions, generally in the summer months. There were firework displays, multi-gun salutes, boating, picnicking, games, and mock naval battles with special crews kept and trained for the purpose. The guests wandered about the park or the formal gardens, where they found pavilions where meals were always ready and there was often an open-air theatre with a permanent serf troupe of singers, dancers and actors. At the end of the century, Peter Sheremetiev's son, Nicholas, fell in love with one of the actresses in the troupe, and married her, for which he was ostracized by the more snobbish element of Moscow society.

The eighteenth-century country house was nearly always sited in a mature park, which could be a formal garden or acres of parkland. In the vicinity of the house there would be flowerbeds, evolved from the vegetable patches of the past, and the layout was often 'in the English style', with avenues in vista form, lined with maple or lime trees, leading from one pavilion to another. There was almost invariably a 'hermitage' or 'belvedere' of some sort, and it was also usual to have an orangery for exotic plants, an aviary and a dovecote over a cellar where ice was stored. The descriptions of some of these houses also list an array of utilitarian outbuildings such as sawmills, breweries, papermills, and of course stables and cattleyards, coach houses and accommodation for a large number of servants – grooms, blacksmiths and leatherworkers, for example. Some estates had their own private porcelain factory, and many of these produced work of international quality. Not far from the big house stood a small church, quite often dating from the time of the original timber house, and often of great architectural interest. If the local architect who was commissioned to build the house was also entrusted with the church, he had a wonderful opportunity to display his originality and demonstrate his artistry and creativity; an example is the excellent Russian architect Matvei (Matthew) Kazakov, who built quite modest houses, but very original churches, at Bykovo and Vinogradovo. (The houses are no longer visible, however.)

At Marfino, some twenty-five miles north of Moscow, is a splendid estate which is a delight today, although undergoing considerable restoration. The picturesque church was built in 1707 by a serf architect, Belozerov, when the estate belonged to Prince Boris Galitzine, who had been tutor to the young Peter I. After Galitzine died the estate remained unoccupied for several years, then passed into the hands of the Saltykovs. During the French invasion of 1812 it suffered at the hands of Napoleon's Grande Armée, was restored by the Orlovs, heirs of the Saltykovs, and then passed into the possession of the Counts Panin, having gone through many architectural changes and neo-Gothic extensions and embellishments. The story is typical of many such houses and estates. In the later period of Russia's industrial development, many notable houses passed into the hands of what were known then as merchants (we would call them industrial magnates today); the interesting colony-estate of Abramtsevo, for example, was bought in 1870 by Savva Mamontov, a great patron of artists, and became a haven for many of the leading artists of the turn of the century.

Since the Second World War the Soviet societies for the preservation of historical monuments of all sorts have done magnificent work in restoring some of the Imperial palaces outside St Petersburg. Other organizations have undertaken the rehabilitation of some country houses outside Moscow, and provincial centres of historical interest have repaired some of the more notable churches and monasteries. One of the outstanding contributions of all this work has been the long overdue removal of various excrescences and so-called improvements made during the Victorian era, resulting in the strict medieval purity, the severe and unadorned simplicity, of churches like the Church of the Intercession of the Virgin on the Nerl river outside Vladimir, or some of the solitary ancient churches in the trading quarter of Novgorod. These are modern creations from ancient remains, restored under the strict control of archaeologists of the Soviet post-war age, and can be regarded as the academic forerunners of *glasnost*.

A recent book on Russian emigrants, published in England, concludes with the following remark: 'What is the relationship of Russian past and Soviet present?' I belong firmly to the first category, and find that I remain endlessly puzzled by the relationship, of which both sides are the victims. Having been born in Russia just before the Bolshevik Revolution, been a regular visitor from the days of Khrushchev, throughout the Brezhnev era, and now a frequent witness of *glasnost* and the ever-swinging pendulum of *perestroika*, I can only persevere, with hope and faith sustained by an atavistic love of the land and people of my forebears, and try to guess the future, and help by interpreting to those puzzled what I think I understand, and appreciate that which I can admire. Kuskovo, Marfino, the palaces of St Petersburg, are tangible witnesses to the high cultural achievement of their times.

My parents started what in Soviet Russia is referred to as 'the first wave of emigration'. Because I left Russia with them as a baby I belong to that wave. There are only a few of us left, but we are the last link with Imperial splendour.

Author's Note

The transliteration of Russian names from the Cyrillic alphabet into Latin letters is often regarded as a problem. There should not be any problem, as no correct solution can possibly exist. One can only agree to use one of the accepted systems. On the whole I favour a system which gives names their most familiar form to English readers. In Russian Peter is *Pyotr*, Catherine is *Yekaterina*, Michael is *Mikhail*. I have favoured the familiar English forms, so as not to shock or puzzle. I am convinced that most English readers prefer to see Tchaikovsky and not *Chaikovski*; Chaliapine and not *Shalyapin*; Nijinsky and not *Nizhinski*.

I have therefore used the familiar version of most first names: e.g. Nicholas (instead of *Nikolai*), where there exists a familiar English version, but I admit to inconsistencies. I have used *Andrei*, instead of Andrew, but Elizabeth instead of *Yelizaveta*.

The spelling of my own family name needs some explanation. Nowadays, Soviet writers spell our name roughly transliterated as *Golitsyn*, but we use the now familiar form – Galitzine – which is the phonetic French version adopted by members of our family in the Corps Diplomatique in the eighteenth century, and which has become accepted as traditional in the family.

I have also used the more modern translation of the Russian title of *Velikiy Kniaz* as Great Prince, instead of Grand Duke, which English writers took over from the French Grand Duc. The only Russian title is *Kniaz* and the adjective *Velikiy* merely qualifies it as Great or Grand. It was applied, with the adjective, to the sons and daughters of the Tsar up to two generations only. The titles of Count (*Graf*) and Baron were taken straight from the German without translation, by Peter the Great onwards.

This book is dedicated to
the spirit of the people of Russia,
past, present and future.

NOVGOROD

After Kiev, Novgorod is the most historic and ancient city in Russia. Several centuries before Moscow became predominant, Novgorod had already established itself as a prosperous trading centre. Although Russian monastic chronicles go back only as far as 1040, there are a wealth of earlier records in the folk sagas and legends known as *byliny*, traditional epic poems recited in a special sing-song tone and handed down from generation to generation, that bear witness to the existence of a city in the land of Rus as long ago as the very beginning of its history.

The first names in Russian history are those of the Varangian (or Viking) warrior merchants, who plied their trade along the Eastern Way from the Baltic and Eastern Europe to Byzantium and the Orient. They travelled along the river routes, using relatively short land links to drag their boats to the next river or lake. Novgorod, situated on the Volkhov river only four miles from Lake Ilmen, was naturally strategically placed to become the Vikings' main trading post in this rich land of opportunity.

For this reason one of the most conspicuous features of the Novgorod Kremlin is the Monument to the Millennium of Russian history, erected in 1862. Exactly 1,000 years before, so the ancient legend goes, the Slavic tribes along the river route appealed to the Varangians to come and protect them from the continual marauding of the Khozars, Pechenegs, Polovtsy and other fierce nomads: 'Our land is vast and fruitful, but there is no order; come and reign and rule over us,' as every Russian child learns. In answer to this invitation came Rurik; he settled in Novgorod, 'New Town', the name probably being given because the city moved from its original site to one further along the river bank soon after the first settlement. Rurik's successors moved south to Kiev, which became the capital of the new state founded by the Varangian leaders. Rurik (in old Norse Hraerekr, which is the same as Roderic) founded a

dynasty which survived until the end of the sixteenth century, and from which the majority of the old Russian aristocratic families derive their origin.

The city of Novgorod lies on both sides of the river Volkhov. On the left side is the Kremlin, surrounded by an imposing castellated red brick wall, with fortification towers, built in the fifteenth century, inside which are the most striking monuments of its history. Foremost among these is the Cathedral of St Sophia, erected by Novgorod's first bishop, Joachim, who was appointed by the Great Prince of Kiev in 989. His first cathedral, a massive oak structure of that date, was destroyed by fire. The present building was started in 1405 under Prince Yaroslav the Wise, a son of Kiev's Prince Vladimir, who baptized the Kievan people into Christianity in the Dnieper river in 988 and was canonized by the Russian Orthodox Church. The cathedral is typical of the Novgorodian style of architecture: it is built of undressed stone, devoid of ornament, and has very few windows – an adaptation designed to suit the colder northern climate. It is intriguing to compare its contemporaries in the West – Durham Cathedral, Westminster Abbey and the cathedrals of Parma and Pisa. Archaeological excavations in Novgorod have provided a great wealth of information about its early history, for such cities have an advantage over those which have had an uninterrupted evolution. Novgorod became a provincial backwater from the beginning of the sixteenth century, with scarcely any important structural additions thereafter. It is therefore a virtual museum city of earliest Russian culture, of the six centuries before Moscow emerged as the dominant capital of Russia, and particularly revealing about the forgotten era prior to the overrunning of the land by the Tartar-Mongols in the mid-thirteenth century. Some of the greatest treasures discovered are a mass of manuscript documents written on strips of birch bark from the eleventh to the fifteenth centuries, giving details

Opposite: Detail on the wall of the Church
of the Saviour in Kovalyovo, Novgorod
(14th century)

of ordinary everyday life in this active trading centre.

Very early on, Novgorod established a special position for itself in the Kievan state. Its prince was the second senior member of the Rurikid family, after the one in Kiev, and as the succession did not depend on primogeniture it meant that every time a ruler died a struggle ensued between his brothers, sons and nephews, amounting to civil war. As a result, Novgorod's rulers loosened their ties with Kiev and rapidly established their independence. When Prince Yaroslav died, the chronicle listed his possessions: there was no mention of Novgorod among them, although the prince had been its ruler until he succeeded his father in Kiev, when he handed it over to his own son. This clearly shows that it was not even regarded as part of the Kievan sovereign possessions. This development towards complete independence grew rapidly through the twelfth and thirteenth centuries, and enabled Novgorod to survive as the foremost trade centre long after Kiev had subsided into relative insignificance, having fallen to the Tartars in 1240.

From the middle of the twelfth century the power of the prince declined. The city was governed by a popular assembly called a *veche*, an oligarchic council of nobles and merchants which became so powerful that it even chose its own prince, as it did all the other dignitaries. There was a well-known saying in Novgorod: 'If the prince was no good, then into the mud with him.' He was in charge of the military, which was there to protect them, and the real rulers of the city-state were the archbishop and the appointed *posadnik* (equivalent to a mayor) in council with the *veche*.

The prince had lost his prime status to such an extent that he no longer had the use of the cathedral in the Kremlin and withdrew to the Yuriev (St George) Monastery, founded in 1030 a couple of miles away. A master builder named Peter (and to know the name of builders in those days was exceptional) erected an imposing church there in 1119 to rival the Kremlin cathedral.

The new St Sophia Cathedral in the Kremlin has five domes, the central one in the shape of a huge warrior's helmet capped by a cross and a dove in bronze. A legend says that as long as the dove sits there, Novgorod will continue to exist. Peter's church in the Yuriev monastery has three domes asymmetrically positioned, and the walls of both churches were decorated with notable frescoes, of which, sadly, only a few have survived the neglect of centuries, the ravages of eighteenth- and nineteenth-century over-painting, and finally the terrible damage of two and a half years of occupation by the Nazi army. Nevertheless, the restoration that has been carried out, starting immediately the war ended, is phenomenal. Most of the well-known churches, both on the Sophia side and on the Market side, have been re-erected in their original form; additions and excrescences added in the nineteenth century have been removed. The names of the city's two sides have been preserved to the present day.

The twelfth century was a period of much important building of churches, each with its own individual character. Galleries were added to three façades of St Sophia's Cathedral, and an array of splendid churches went up in the quarters on both sides of the river. Between 1103 and 1207, the informative chronicler tells us, a total of sixty-eight churches were erected. The names of the founders of forty-one of them are given; six were initiated by the prince in the first thirty-two years, and four in the last seventy-three – an eloquent demonstration of the decline of the prince's power. Sixteen of these churches were sponsored by the archbishops, and many others, particularly on the trading side, by wealthy individual merchants or guilds. It is also interesting that on four separate occasions foreign merchants sponsored churches designed to accommodate the Latin rite, emphasizing Novgorod's membership of the Hanseatic League at its Eastern outpost. Whereas it had taken twenty years to build St Sophia's Cathedral in the eleventh century, the average time taken to build these latter churches was only three years (and in one case only seventy days).

All this gave an added dimension to the flourishing trade and wealth of Novgorod, and its territory soon extended from the White Sea in the north, to the Ural mountains in the east, and the Great Principality of Lithuania and the Baltic to the west. It was a true 'window on the west', many centuries before the foundation of St Petersburg. Such fame, wealth and respect were not achieved by trade alone without many a struggle and conquest. Attacks and encroachments from the Suzdal-Vladimir princes alternated regularly with raids by Swedish, Lithuanian and Mongol forces. At the same time the Volkhov Republic itself engaged in many expeditions and annexations. It acquired the name of 'the Lord Novgorod the Great', and a noted saying of the time was: 'Who can stand against God and the Great Novgorod?' A famous battle of the early eleventh century is graphically depicted in a well-known ikon now in the Kremlin Museum. Novgorod was being attacked by the Suzdal Prince Andrei Bogoliubsky, and the ikon painter shows how the defenders of the city brought their most revered ikon, of Our Lady of the Sign, on to the Kremlin walls. In spite of being showered by Suzdalian arrows, the ikon remained unharmed and tears appeared to fall from the Virgin Mary's eyes. This so disconcerted the attackers that they withdrew, and Novgorod was saved. Another version of this ikon is in the Russian Museum in Leningrad.

The mid-thirteenth century saw the devastating invasion of the Tartar-Mongol Golden Horde under Khan Batu, grandson of Ghengis Khan. This was the most profound catastrophe in the history of Russia, and had far-reaching effects. Novgorod and Pskov escaped the destruction and the humiliation of defeat suffered by the other principalities throughout the land of Rus. Exceptionally heavy floods around Novgorod in the spring of 1238 undoubtedly contributed to their salvation, as did the remoteness of their position, particularly that of Pskov. However, the brilliant leadership of Prince Alexander, son of Yaroslav II of Suzdal, was the decisive factor which saved Novgorod from the Tartars' normally invincible onslaught. It was Prince Alexander who earned the title of 'Nevsky' (of the Neva) for his defeat of the Swedes by the river Neva in 1240, and who two years later again won renown by beating a strong army of Teutonic knights on the ice of the frozen Lake Peipus.

Under Alexander's leadership, combined with the long commercial experience and skill of the Novgorod people, a treaty was successfully negotiated with the Tartar Khanate whereby they remained unmolested after the initial offensive had struck their neighbours. After some twenty years Alexander advised that they should pay the tribute demanded to keep them unharmed, and so be able to pursue their profitable trading and continue as the centre of cultural activities, chief among which was the very active and original school of ikon painting. Novgorod and Pskov were the only cities with a powerful and wealthy merchant class who were capable of patronizing the arts, and these were the primary instigators of all the formidable architectural activity which has left such a magnificent heritage today.

Among the most prestigious works of art in Novgorod are the fourteenth-century frescoes on the walls of the churches. Because of their regular contact with Europe through trade, the first powerful waves of the Renaissance were felt and manifested in Novgorod not only from Italy, but from Byzantium, Serbia and the lands around and beyond the Caucasian range of mountains. The greatest artist of the age was Theophanes the Greek, who came from Constantinople and decorated the walls of some forty stone churches throughout Russia during the thirty years that he lived there. Andrei Rublev, without doubt the most admired of all Russian ikon painters, who was a monk at the Trinity Monastery of St Sergius, spent his earliest days working under Theophanes' influence, although there is no actual evidence that he was his pupil. The most famous creations of Theophanes visible today are the frescoes in the Church of the Transfiguration of the Saviour, on Ilyin Street in Novgorod. The frescoes have been painstakingly restored in recent years, and the work still continues.

The fourteenth century witnessed the emergence of the Moscow Great Principality as the dominant power, striving to unite the warring rival principalities under its leadership. During this struggle Novgorod's archbishops bitterly resisted Moscow's claims to supremacy. Foremost among them for many years was Archbishop Euphemius (1429–58), who was responsible for the fine Palace, or rather Hall, of Facets, built in 1433, which was to be the scene more than 100 years later of a

fearful bloodbath under Ivan the Terrible. This archbishop was succeeded by one Iona, who favoured union with Muscovy. With the accession of Ivan III, Moscow's pressure on Novgorod intensified. He spread discord among the boyars, merchants and clergy in the city, with the result that many influential factions gave him their support. Archbishop Iona built an important new church dedicated to the favourite saint of Moscow, Sergei of Radonezh. However, the prince in command of their army stood out against Ivan.

In 1471 Ivan marched against Novgorod supported by the Tartar army and inflicted a severe defeat in the battle of Shelonya, thereby asserting his authority over the 'crowned republic'. Nevertheless opposition continued. The wealthy widow of the *posadnik*, Martha Boretzkaya, led the anti-Moscow faction and tried to enlist the active support of the vigorous King Kazimir IV of Poland. All building in the city was suspended and all resources were concentrated on the struggle. Ivan returned in 1478 and captured the city, carrying off its most prominent citizens as well as the *veche* bell, symbol of their independence, which is still in the Moscow arsenal today. In addition, in order to show his displeasure at the affront he had received from a member of the Hanseatic League, Ivan III had all the foreign merchants put in chains and confiscated their property. The remainder fled. From that date the prosperity of Novgorod rapidly declined. The great city-state, which at one time was able to muster a force of 40,000 men at arms, was said to have a population of only 4,000 and sank into provincial obscurity. It was Ivan III who had the walls of the Novgorod Kremlin rebuilt, however, concurrently with those of Moscow, giving them their current appearance, and various efforts have been made over the centuries to keep the buildings in a state worthy of a historic city of the past.

The remainder of the fifteenth and most of the sixteenth century saw several attempts to revive Novgorod's proud independence, but these invariably led to punitive action from Moscow, followed by deportations and a repopulation action by Muscovites. The final indignity came in 1570, when Tsar Ivan IV, the Terrible, sent in his dreaded *oprichnina* to carry out a veritable massacre among the lesser nobles, merchants and peasants, as well as to ransack monasteries. The terror lasted over six weeks, and the pretext was that the people had been negotiating with the Poles and their Catholic priests. It was said that the river Volkhov was so choked with corpses that it has never frozen at that point since.

Under Peter the Great an attempt was made to replan the layout of the streets in the Market quarter, but this was not carried out effectively until 1778, under Catherine the Great. The result was that some of the churches of the medieval period now stand in odd relationships to the streets, while the clearance operations have revealed some valuable archaeological data.

Previous page: The St Sophia Cathedral.
Novgorod

Above: The Millennium Monument

The St Sophia Cathedral

The Belfry of St Sophia Cathedral

Gatefold: The Kremlin walls of Novgorod

Above: The Church of the Holy Trinity in the
Monastery of the Holy Ghost

Previous page: The Church of Sts Peter and
Paul in Slavno

Above: The St Seplira Cathedral

Above: The Yuriev Monastery

Overleaf: The Church of Sts Peter and Paul
in Kozhevniki

PSKOV

Visitors to the historic city of Pskov nowadays go there for four reasons: to see one of the most picturesque ancient Russian cities of the medieval period; to visit the remains of the heroic tenth-century fortress of Izborsk and appreciate the spectacular countryside; to visit one of Russia's best-known monasteries, at Pechora, which has not been interrupted in its functioning since its foundation in the fifteenth century; and to make a pilgrimage from Pskov to Mikhailovskoe, the family home of Russia's greatest and most beloved poet, Alexander Pushkin, and visit the neighbouring places connected with his name, including the Sviatogorsky Monastery, where he is buried. This pilgrimage is undertaken by hundreds of thousands of Russians every year.

Pskov belongs very much to the pre-Muscovy period of Russian history, and during its early life was part of the Novgorodian principality. It was known as Novgorod's younger brother. First mentioned in the chronicles of the first part of the tenth century, excavations show that there was a settlement of the Slavic Krivich tribe there as far back as the sixth century. When Rurik came in 862 to rule over the Slavic people, tradition says, he was accompanied by two other Vikings, Sineus and Truvor. Sineus went to Bielo-Ozero and Truvor went to Pskov. The spectacular ruins of Izborsk castle, some twenty miles·west of Pskov, have always been connected locally with Truvor's name. In the woods on the hill, among the ruins and remnants of ramparts, there is now a cemetery, and prominent among the crosses is a massive stone one supposed to be Truvor's cross. However, archaeologists have established that it dates back to the sixteenth century, possibly the fifteenth at the earliest, and is therefore most likely a communal cross for a military grave, one of the inevitable results of the continual attacks which such an outpost would repeatedly suffer from its western neighbours, the Swedes, Poles, Lithuanians and Teutonic knights.

In many ways Pskov's history followed a similar pattern to that of Novgorod. They were both primarily merchant centres whose origins arose from their geographical position and from their native product, flax. Pskov, besides being situated at the confluence of two rivers, the wide Velikaya and its smaller tributary the Pskova, is in an area of large lakes leading straight into the Baltic Sea. As a direct result of their location, both cities rose to become mighty emporia through trade between Europe and Byzantium. Both became members of the Hanseatic League. Neither city suffered from the Tartar-Mongol invasions, and at different periods they both had the same political structure – a merchant republic administered by a *veche*, though Pskov differed slightly in that its *veche* elected two *posadniks*, who operated as mayor and judge. Finally, both cities have a wealth of ancient monuments, particularly medieval churches.

Pskov's history falls into three distinct sections. The first period runs from its foundation to the Treaty of Volotov (1348), by which Novgorod recognized Pskov's independence; the second period covers Pskov as an independent merchant republic and lasts up to the beginning of the sixteenth century; and the third runs from the time when Pskov, no longer able to resist Moscow's spreading supremacy, joined the Great Prince of Moscow and developed as the western outpost of the Muscovite empire, and continues until the creation of St Petersburg took over the trading activities of both Novgorod and Pskov in their relations with western Europe.

The heart of Pskov is of course the Kremlin – the Krom, as it is known locally. In the middle is the magnificent Trinity Cathedral, with its five domes and its commanding position. It was founded in 1138 but its present appearance dates from the very end of the seventeenth century. The Krom proved almost impregnable, with its triangular shape on a steep hill protected on two sides by the rivers Velikaya and Pskova, and a deep moat called the Greblya joining the rivers. In its time, Pskov withstood twenty-six sieges from its western enemies, and only once, in 1240, did the attackers succeed in entering the Krom, and that was because a treacherous member of the *veche* let them in. In 1242, however, St Alexander Nevsky fought his famous battle on the ice of Lake Peipus (Chudskoe in Russian), thoroughly routing the Knights of the Teutonic Order, and the invading Germans no longer posed a threat. It was in the Trinity Cathedral that Alexander Nevsky was publicly acclaimed.

Pskov's greatest hero, also later canonized among the saints in the Russian Orthodox calendar, was Prince Dovmont, who fled from his native Lithuania, where he was being persecuted by hostile rivals, and who was Pskov's prince for thirty-three triumphant years, from 1266–99, defending the city against numerically superior forces in a series of brilliant victories. Dovmont's sword used to hang over his tomb in the Trinity Cathedral, and later princes were invested with it at their coronation ceremony. It now hangs in the local museum. Other figures connected with Pskov's history are also commemorated in the cathedral. There is Princess Olga, who ruled the land of Rus after her husband, Prince Igor's, death had left her as Regent for her small son, Rurik's grandson. She was a simple girl from Pskov according to historic legend, and is buried in

the Trinity Cathedral. Also commemorated is the first prince of the Rurikid line, Vsevolod, who died in 1138 and under whose reign the first stone version of the cathedral was founded.

Pskov builders achieved renown in the Middle Ages, and after they had been obliged to recognize the supremacy of Moscow, Great Prince Ivan III summoned masters there to assist with his building programme. Their building technique, particular to Pskov, was dictated by the materials available. They used rough limestone and set boulders of it in thick mortar, covering the surface with plaster until it was more or less uniform, then colouring the whole. The effect is like an uneven stucco. The windows are in the form of loopholes and their small size emphasizes the vast expanse of the wall surfaces. The walls are not strictly vertical, many having the effect of swelling towards the lower end, but the result is pleasing because of the light and shade on the wall surfaces.

The citizens of Pskov used to build together without necessarily having any special training, so they kept their aims as simple as possible and the effect is of making all the buildings feel like cosy dwellings. This is particularly true with the churches of the merchants of the fifteenth and sixteenth centuries. The typical Pskov church would have a single drum on the roof supporting the dome; this sometimes contained

the belfry, although it was more usual to put a belfry on a separate wall specially built for the bells. A massive belfry might also be erected near the church it was serving. The single-domed Church of the Holy Ghost at the Trinity Monastery of St Sergius outside Moscow was constructed by Pskov builders, and the most famous example of Pskov architecture is the Cathedral of St Basil the Blessed in Red Square in Moscow, whose architect was Postnik Yakovlev, of whom the story is told that Ivan the Terrible had his eyes put out so that he would not be able to build another like it for anyone else. (This story is also told about the Taj Mahal at Agra, as well as several other unique buildings.)

Besides the Pechora Monastery, there are two other ancient monasteries at Pskov which are specially notable. The Mirozhsky Monastery was founded in the middle of the twelfth century by Archbishop Nifont of Novgorod and Pskov (the see was combined until Pskov became independent), and its frescoes, painted by Greek artists and their Russian pupils, are in a remarkably good state of preservation. This is probably due largely to their having been whitewashed over in the eighteenth century and discovered accidentally in the nineteenth. The frescoes in the cathedral of this monastery are some of the most remarkable works of art in the whole of Russia.

The other monastery has only a single church left. This is the Ivanovsky Cathedral, dating from the twelfth century, which is all that remains of the Ivanovsky Convent, mentioned in the chronicles of 1243. Here, over many hundred years of its history, the princesses of Pskov were buried. In the seventeenth century many merchant families built important and attractive houses which have remained, together with the names of their owners. Some four miles outside the city is the Snetogorsky Monastery, which dates from the fourteenth century, with alterations from the seventeenth. Its interesting early fourteenth-century frescoes have now been restored, and show unusual themes from apocryphal legends and themes rather than the usual gospel subjects.

Sadly, Pskov is also remembered for the final tragic gesture of the last Romanov Tsar, Nicholas II, who signed the instrument of abdication in his railway carriage on the way back from his operational headquarters to St Petersburg (Petrograd as it was then) on 15 March 1917, in the presence of two emissaries from the capital who had been sent to persuade him to sign. Pskov was thus an accidental witness to the end of the monarchy in Russia.

Previous page: The Pechora Monastery

Above: The Pechora Monastery
Overleaf: The Mirozhsky Monastery

Gatefold: View of the Kremlin across the
Velikaya river

Above: The Ivanov Cathedral on the
Vazelichye

Previous page: The Kremlin

Above: The Izborsk Fortress

The Fortress Tower

The Church of St John the Baptist

GOLDEN RING

The Golden Ring is the name given to a tourist journey, consisting of a group of ancient and historic Russian cities starting with Moscow and fanning out towards the north-east. The route takes in cities and villages of old Muscovy, each one of which has its own particular place in history. Most of the buildings are ecclesiastical, since these are the only stone buildings from the Middle Ages which have survived. All are situated by the rivers which linked the Baltic with the Black Sea and Byzantium, the centre of the world as it was then. Many of these cities were flourishing commercial centres developed from pre-Slav tribal settlements, and were in regular trading contact with Constantinople and the Western world before the Tartar-Mongol invasion interrupted their lives.

Nearly every city of the Golden Ring has a citadel – a Kremlin – with a church, often called a cathedral, at its centre. They have fortifications in varying degrees of preservation, perhaps part of a city wall and ramparts, several monasteries, always fortified, and sometimes signs of city gates, but seldom any secular buildings. The countryside is flat and densely forested, with lakes as well as rivers affecting the location of the key buildings. The cities in the north form a nucleus of the Great Russian State which was evolving before the Tartar-Mongol invasion, and which was eventually to come under the domination of Moscow after Kiev lost its supremacy among the Great Princes. The Golden Ring is continually being expanded, and it is possible to mention only a few sites here.

The first mention of Suzdal in the monastic chronicles occurs in 1024. Towards the end of the eleventh century the Suzdal lands became part of the territory of Prince Vladimir Monomakh, Great Prince of Kiev, who was married to Ghyta, daughter of King Harold of England. Suzdal was an important northern outpost, and the Prince built ramparts and other fortifications to defend the trading and artisan settlement, including the first Christian stone church. His son, Prince Yuri Dolgoruky, further developed the city and surrounding lands and made Suzdal the capital of his principality in 1125. He and his son, Prince Andrei Bogoliubsky, fought many campaigns in the area to defend their patrimony. Prince Yuri aspired to establish his rule in the most senior seat in Kiev, where he died in 1157. He is also regarded as the founder of Moscow itself, which has its first mention in 1147. Prince Andrei renounced his succession to the principality of Kiev, and later overran it with an armed force, thereby confirming the position of Vladimir as the new capital of Rus and underlining the lapse of Kiev from its supremacy. The northern principality was variously known as the Rostov-Suzdal, or sometimes the Suzdal-Vladimir, principality. As further confirmation, Prince Andrei brought the most sacred Byzantine ikon of the Virgin and Child, which originally came from Constantinople, from Kiev to Vladimir. Since then it has been known as the Virgin of Vladimir, and it is Russia's most venerated ikon. When it was transferred to Moscow many years later this was done as final emphasis that the supremacy had gone to that city.

The ancient chronicles vividly describe many aspects of Prince Andrei's turbulent reign and forceful character. He made his home a few miles outside Vladimir at Bogoliubovo, where a part of his secular palace building remains, although most of it was destroyed by the Tartar-Mongols in the thirteenth century. During his eventful reign, Vladimir's most notable building, the Cathedral of the Assumption of the Virgin (or Dormition), was erected in 1158–60. It stands on the steep banks overlooking the river Klyazma, and was to rival both in beauty and in sumptuousness the great cathedral of St Sophia at Kiev. The chronicles praise the gilded dome flashing in the sunlight, and the brightness of the copper blind arcading. The presence inside of the famous ikon ensured the cathedral's status as the foremost in the land. The ikon is now permanently on view in the Tretyakov Art Gallery in Moscow, together with

Opposite: Sunrise over Suzdal

some of the most outstanding works of Andrei Rublev, whose frescoes in the same cathedral have recently been restored and are an important feature of medieval Russian art.

The cathedral suffered a terrible fire in 1185, and Prince Andrei's son, Vsevolod 'Big Nest' (given his nickname because of his numerous family), rebuilt it almost entirely, enlarging its size and adding four cupolas, one at each corner, making five in all. A gallery between the old and new walls was built, which houses the tombs of local dignitaries, including those of the rulers. (Three hundred years later, Moscow's Prince Ivan III, the Great, sent Aristotle Fioravanti, whom he had hired from Bologna in Italy to come and build the major stone cathedral in the Moscow Kremlin, to Vladimir to study the Dormition Cathedral there, and learn the ritual requirements of the Russian Orthodox church.)

The other architectural treasure built under Prince Vsevolod was the unique single-domed Cathedral of St Dmitri, erected in 1197. Its rich relief carvings of birds, foliage, saints, kings, prophets and animals are impressive at close quarters. The outstanding memorial to that period in the area is the Church of the Intercession of the Virgin on the Nerl river, dating from 1165, invariably referred to as a real jewel of architecture. It stands alone, next to a lake which is part of the river, surrounded by a few elms, across an open watermeadow. Its proportions are of extreme simplicity and quite faultless, and in its solitary situation it dazzles with its breathtaking beauty. One year earlier, Prince Andrei had built the Golden Gates at the entrance through the ramparts surrounding the city of Vladimir. This rare secular structure still stands, although altered through the ages, as a reminder of the martial nature of these cities of the Golden Ring. It is a combination of a fortified tower commanding access to the city and a triumphal arch for the celebration of official ceremonies such as greeting the return of an army, or its departure. The gates themselves consisted of massive oak doors clad in gilded copper, which was stripped off by the victorious Tartars in the thirteenth century. Inside the tall central arch was a platform of wooden beams, for the defenders to stand on and pour boiling water or oil on their attackers. When Khan Batu's army attacked Vladimir in 1238, they failed to gain entry through the gate in spite of repeated attempts. They finally got in through holes blown by artillery in the wooden palisade walls. These same gates also withstood bombardment from Polish-Lithuanian cannon during the memorable siege in the early 1600s, during the Time of Troubles, prior to the election of the first Romanov Tsar.

Suzdal's history is less turbulent. With its emblem, the falcon, it is more reminiscent of an old Russian fairy tale. After the fall of Kiev, Suzdal became the religious centre of medieval Rus. Its Cathedral of the Nativity of the Virgin displays some of Russia's earliest stone foundations, but it is most famous for two 'golden' doors from the thirteenth century, made with a

'damascening' technique. It also has some frescoes from the same period, and a splendid late seventeenth-century ikonastasis (altar screen).

In the early part of the twelfth century, when Prince Yuri Dolgoruky made Suzdal his capital, he chose to live for part of the time a few miles away at Kideksha, where all approaches were easily visible from afar, giving him good warning of any enemy who might come to assassinate him. By early the next century Suzdal was an independent principality, and in an attempt to preserve this status it combined with Nizhni-Novgorod, a very ancient trading centre. However, this resistance to Moscow's growing supremacy collapsed at the end of the fourteenth century; Suzdal lost its political importance and retained only its religious influence.

In the sixteenth century, building resumed when a number of churches were ordered by the Muscovite Great Prince Vassily III and his son, the youthful Ivan IV, the Terrible, who assumed the title of Tsar in 1547 at the age of seventeen. There are many monasteries in Suzdal, but two in particular stand

out, contrasting both in appearance and in their history. One is named after its founder, as the Saviour and St Euphemius. It has massive red brick walls and looks fearful and forbidding. The other, a white-walled building in a valley across the river, is the Convent of the Intercession of the Virgin. The former was used as a corrective establishment for recalcitrant priests who were regarded as having dangerous ideas contrary to the teachings of the Church, and later became a prison for all sorts of political prisoners. Its belfry, however, housed a carillon of wonderful bells whose peals are a great attraction for visitors.

The Convent of the Intercession, on the other hand, has a more intriguing story. In Moscow there is a small and well-known church outside the Kremlin called St Anne-What's-in-the-Corner. It was a place of pilgrimage for barren wives, who used to come there to pray to St Anne, who was herself barren for a long time and then gave birth to the future John the Baptist. Early in the sixteenth century the wife of the Great Prince Vassily III, Solomonia Saburova, found herself unable to produce a son and heir for him, and her husband spent many

years negotiating to divorce her, with little success. Then one day he fell in love with a young Polish girl called Yelena (Helen) Glinska, whom he wished to marry, but because she was a Roman Catholic his advisers, the Duma, and the Metropolitan of Moscow were all strongly opposed to this plan. On returning to the Kremlin one day after having been to pray to St Anne, Solomonia learned that Vassily was planning to banish her to the convent in Suzdal, but her prayers had been answered and some months after arriving at her place of exile, she gave birth to a son. When the news reached Moscow, the Great Prince sent emissaries to Suzdal to confirm the rumour. Solomonia, hearing that they were approaching and fearing for her child's life, staged a mock funeral, saying that the boy had died. The Muscovites returned to their sovereign and reported that the child had indeed been born, but that he had died and that they had witnessed his burial. According to local legend, Solomonia arranged for the boy to be adopted in Suzdal. Years later it was rumoured that a notorious leader of an outlaw band who carried out regular robberies of the rich and helped the local poor, in the manner of Robin Hood, was that same young son of Solomonia. In Soviet times, Solomonia's tomb and that of her child were opened, and the latter was found to contain only a rag doll.

Other notable cities of the Golden Ring are the very ancient cities of Yaroslavl, Uglich and Kostroma, each with its own particular character and high point in history. At Uglich, the young Tsarevich Dmitri died in mysterious circumstances in 1591. The Tsar, Boris Godunov, was suspected of having had him murdered and the Time of Troubles which followed led to the election of young Michael Romanov in 1613. Michael was living at Kostroma with his mother when he heard that the Boyars' Assembly (dominated by elders of the Dolgoruky and Galitzine families) had decided to elect him to the throne. At Kostroma, too, a merchant engaged in trade with England discovered some gold pieces in a barrel of dyes. He wrote to England about his discovery and asked what to do with the gold. The English company replied that it should be used for good works, and the result was a beautiful church which is one of the finest examples of seventeenth-century architecture in Russia and has a lion and a unicorn on the outside as evidence of the story.

The churches in the Suzdal area were often built in pairs, with a free-standing belfry serving both churches. One church would be high-vaulted and elaborately decorated, for summer use, the other small and more simple for winter; although neither was heated, the smaller church was usually the more comfortable, with candles and sanctuary lamps creating the illusion of warmth and cosiness. This arrangement of paired churches is also found just outside the walls of the Trinity Monastery of St Sergius at Zagorsk, about forty-six miles north of Moscow, which is the first centre to be reached from

Moscow on the Golden Ring circuit.

The Trinity Monastery of St Sergius

The Trinity Monastery of St Sergius (Sergei in Russian) at Zagorsk (a town named after a revolutionary killed in 1919 by an anarchist's bomb) is a spectacular fortress complex of medieval ecclesiastical buildings, surrounded by formidable walls with defensive towers. The gold of the typical Russian cupola domes shines in the sun as you approach, and four of the domes of the main cathedral dazzle you with golden stars on a dark blue background.

Monasteries have played a special role in the history of Russia, and the Trinity Monastery of St Sergius contributed more than any other to the emergence of Moscow as the leading principality of central and northern Russia in the late fourteenth and early fifteenth centuries. The many monasteries spread across the country helped significantly in the colonization process of that enormous territory. They were strong military and feudal centres, and at the same time unique focuses for culture and education at a time when these functions could not be performed by government.

The Trinity Monastery, founded in the middle of the fourteenth century, was one of the earliest, and was the vital nucleus of a whole system of such monasteries. Its founder, Sergei of Radonezh, was a man of remarkable personality. Born in about 1319 into a noble family of Rostov, he and his elder brother decided to retire from society into the forest and live a life of prayer and contemplation. They built a church of wood, and invited a priest to come and consecrate it in the name of the Holy Trinity. Very soon news of Sergei's virtues and personality spread afar, and pilgrims came to follow his way of life. He tried hard to conceal his feats, but rumour attracted a dozen pious men who came to lead their lives in devotion and prayer under his guidance. They built their cells around the little wooden church and so, in 1340, the Trinity Monastery was established.

As abbot of the Trinity Monastery since 1354, Sergei of Radonezh established a new order there. Instead of each monk fending only for himself, Sergei organized them so that all activity should be performed for the common good. The monastery was situated on the main road to Moscow from the northern cities, and all kinds of people, high and low, came to him for advice and guidance, at the same time bestowing gifts and bequests, until very soon Sergei's fame reached even Constantinople and the Patriarch there. The powerful Metropolitan Alexis, the primate and archbishop of Moscow – like Sergei also later canonized – esteemed him greatly and entrusted him with all manner of difficult missions, in particular those involving peacemaking among the feuding rival princes.

Sergei earned himself the title in Russian history of 'Protector of the Land', and has always been Russia's favourite patron saint. He convinced the princes that when divided and warring with each other they were an easy prey for the Tartar Khanate, but united they could be more than a match for the Golden Horde, which by then had begun to be torn by internal discord. When Ivan Kalita's most able successor, Dmitri Ivanovich, became Great Prince of Moscow in 1363, Sergei worked closely with him to free the Russian people from the Tartar suzerainty. Sergei established a ring of fortified monasteries to the south of Moscow, expanding the order established by himself. At last Prince Dmitri felt strong and determined enough to challenge Khan Mamai, but first he marched his army and the princes with their hosts to be blessed by Sergei at the Trinity Monastery. Sergei sent two of his most stalwart monks, Peresviet and Oslabia, both well versed in the martial arts of the time, to accompany the Muscovite force. They reached the banks of the river Don two days before the feast of the Birthday of the Virgin Mary, and then began, on 8 September 1380, the famous and bloody battle of Kulikovo Field. At the very start, Brother Peresviet came out and challenged Khan Mamai to send out his champion, Temir Mirza, into single combat with him. Both sides suffered terrible casualties, but at last Khan Mamai withdrew what remained of his hitherto victorious army. Both Peresviet and Oslabia perished, but Prince Dmitri had at last demonstrated to the Russian people and to their leaders once and for all that Tartar-Mongol invincibility was a myth.

After the battle, Dmitri went back to the Trinity Monastery to thank Sergei for his prayers on their behalf, and for the part he had played in exhorting the princes, without threats and without coercion, to sacrifice their own interests and unite against the common enemy. Sergei's reputation grew and flourished. His monastery received more gifts, privileges and donations of valuable treasures, as well as hundreds of serfs, to the extent that a special appointment was created to manage its affairs and interests.

Sergei of Radonezh died in 1392. In 1406 Khan Yedigei attacked the monastery and reduced it to ashes, but Nikon, the abbot, enlisting the ready support of Moscow's Great Prince, quickly rebuilt the wooden Trinity Cathedral and the cells.

In 1422 Sergei was canonized, and a new Trinity Cathedral in white limestone was erected over his tomb in place of the timber one. It was built in the Suzdal-Vladimir style with a single dome, and completed in 1427; this is the cathedral which stands today. The monastery continued to flourish, and became the scene of many dramatic episodes in the fifteenth century. The Great Princes of Russia's young capital, Moscow, had their sons and heirs brought there for baptism. Vassily III was baptized there in 1479, and so were his son Ivan the Terrible, in 1530, and Ivan's two sons in their turn. Vassily announced his victory over the city of Pskov in 1540 with a triumphal peal of the monastery bells, as did his son after he captured Kazan from the Tartars in 1532, when he emulated the example of Dmitri of the Don and went specially to the Trinity Monastery of St Sergius before marching on his successful campaign against the Khanates of Kazan and Astrakhan. On his return he made a point of calling at the monastery to celebrate his victory.

The greatest artistic contribution from the Trinity Monastery was in the field of ikon painting, which reached its apogee in the fifteenth century. The Trinity Cathedral was decorated with frescoes and ikons by two monks, Daniel Chorny and Andrei Rublev; the latter's world-famous ikon of the Old Testament Trinity was painted for the altar screen (ikonastasis) of the new Trinity Cathedral (the ikon is now in the Tretyakov Art Gallery in Moscow, and a copy occupies its original place).

The monastery, as a foundation, kept growing in wealth and prestige in the most remarkable way, in spite of the many setbacks it was destined to suffer. Its largest central cathedral, the Assumption of the Virgin Mary, was begun in the reign of Ivan the Terrible, in 1559. It has five onion-shaped domes; the central one is covered in gold leaf and the four around it are painted dark blue with gold stars. It was consecrated in 1589, and also commemorates the conquests of Kazan and Astrakhan by Ivan the Terrible.

At the beginning of the seventeenth century, even before the death of the Tsar Boris Godunov in 1605, Russia went through a decade of what is known in her history as 'the Time of Troubles'. Several pretenders claiming to be Ivan the Terrible's son, Dmitri, who was supposed to have died in 1591, came forward and claimed that they were the rightful heirs to the Muscovite throne. The first Dmitri was backed by Catholic Poland and Lithuania, and was soon joined by some powerful nobles and an army of mercenary Cossacks. The Trinity Monastery remained loyal to the old order and guarded the road to the northern cities. The Pretender's army, under the command of the Polish Prince Peter Sapieha and Alexander Lissovsky, laid siege to the monastery with a force of some 15,000 warriors. Although the monastery had only about 2,500 defenders, not counting 1,000 unarmed local citizens who had taken refuge within its walls, they refused to surrender, and the siege dragged on for sixteen bitter months, until the Poles finally gave up and withdrew their armies.

The Pretender was finally captured in Moscow and killed. His mutilated body, exposed to the public gaze for three days, was finally burned, and the ashes were loaded into a cannon and fired towards Poland. Prince Ivan Shuysky then usurped the throne, but proved too weak to restore order. A second pseudo-Dmitri threatened Moscow and the Polish occupants of the Kremlin. When chaos and anarchy were at their worst, the Trinity Monastery led a religious revival to save Orthodox Russia from foreign and Catholic rule. From the stronghold of the monastery came Father Abram Palitzyn, who went round

the villages and towns preaching and inspiring Russian folk to rise up and defend their land from foreign invaders. A national Council met, under the authority of the Suzdal prince Dmitri Pozharsky and of Kuzma Minin, a butcher of Nizhni-Novgorod, and they raised a people's army, which proceeded to drive the Poles out of Moscow and put an end to this strife-torn period.

The Council was composed of several factions of the powerful boyars, dominated by Dolgorukys and Galitzines, whose rival interests had torn the country over the last years by backing and opposing the various claimants. What was clearly needed was a focus for all their loyalties, and under the direction of the Church leaders, chief of whom was the abbot of the Trinity Monastery, the Council, with the vociferous support of the mercenary Cossack leaders and other military elements, elected the sixteen-year-old Michael Romanov, son of the influential Metropolitan Filaret, to occupy the vacant throne. Michael was seriously daunted by the prospect, but soon after his reign began, his father was released from imprisonment at the hands of the Poles and ruled the country jointly with his son as Patriarch of the Orthodox Church. One of the first actions of the new Tsar was to pay a visit to the Trinity Monastery of St Sergius, to receive the blessing of the saint for his reign.

In the later part of the seventeenth century the monastery twice gave refuge to the young boy Tsar Peter, who became Peter the Great and Russia's first Emperor. On the first occasion he had to flee there with his half-sister Sophia and her brother, Ivan V, his co-Tsar, from a plot by the mutinous Streltsy (or Musketeers) under their commander, Prince Khovansky. The second time, Peter arrived at the monastery alone, having galloped from Moscow to escape from a *coup d'état* engineered by Sophia, who was acting as Regent. In 1689 Peter took over the reigns of power; Sophia was banished to a convent, and the Trinity Monastery donated 400,000 roubles – an enormous sum at the time – for Peter to equip his army for the war against Sweden, and to build a fleet, as well as to finance his radical reforms.

In the eighteenth century, the talented Russian architect Prince Ukhtomsky erected the beautiful belfry and circular church of the Virgin of Smolensk, after important repairs to the older buildings following a serious fire in 1746. The same century also saw the addition of spacious buildings to house the Theological College, which is there now, and the living quarters of the Metropolitan. Apart from its religious legacy, the Trinity Monastery of St Sergius always used its enormous riches and power to further the good of the country. In years of famine and plague and other disasters, it invariably opened the doors of its thirty-four monasteries to thousands of hungry and needy people throughout the country. Altogether the monastery's contribution to the general cultural development of Russia is beyond measure.

Above: The Archbishop's Palace, Suzdal

Overleaf: Kideksha across the Nerl river,
Suzdal

The Gatehouse, Convent of the
Intercession of the Virgin

The Posad House (c.1700) and the Church
of the Virgin of Smolensk

Gatefold: Suzdal

Above: Church by old rampart

The Church of the Transfiguration from
Kozliatevo village (1756)

Previous page: Suzdal from old rampart

The Church of St Nicholas from Glotovo
village (1766)

Overleaf: The Monastery of St Alexander
Nevsky

The Church of the Intercession of the Holy
Virgin on the Nerl river (1165)

The Cathedral of the Assumption

Above and gatefold: The Cathedral of the Assumption, Trinity Monastery of St Sergius

Above: The Smolensky Church and
Hospital, Trinity Monastery of St Sergius

Overleaf: Cupolas of the Trinity Monastery
of St Sergius

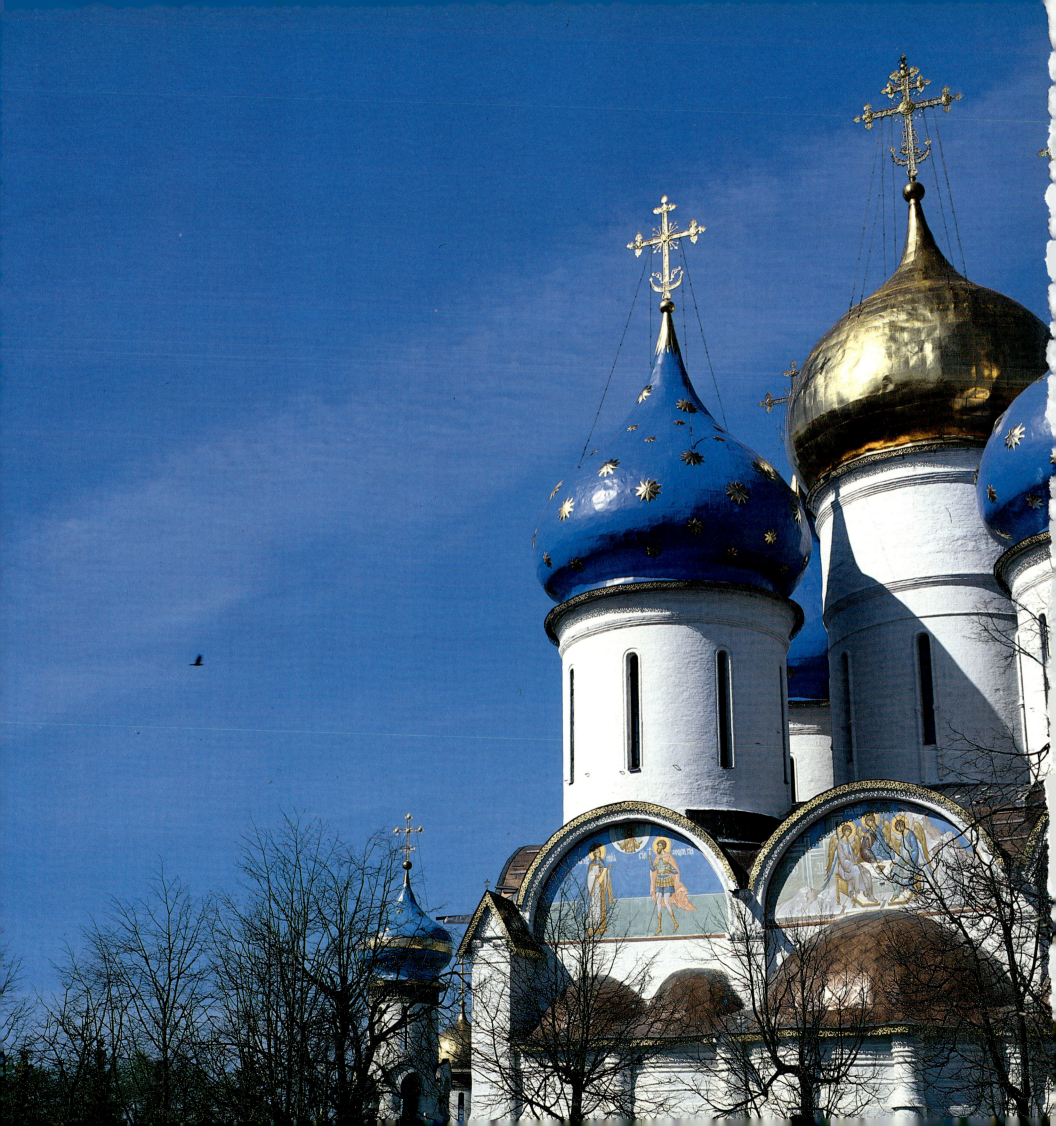

MOSCOW

A first visit to Moscow can be decidedly disappointing. Even if you are very open-minded you cannot help but feel that the streets are unimpressive and the buildings unglamorous, with no particular character or style. It is quite unlike the first impression of St Petersburg, for example, with its expanse of water and the spectacular architecture in the centre of the city. Yet Moscow soon begins to grow on you, and the more you look, the more you find intriguing. As you approach the heart of Moscow, you see the massive red walls of the Kremlin, the glint of gold from the domes and cupolas of the cathedrals, and then the wide expanse of Red Square, with the fairy-tale shapes and colours of St Basil's Church at one end overlooking the Moskva river.

The city of Moscow is not only the heart but emphatically the very soul of Russia, as is soon learned from its history. The first mention of the city was in 1147, when Prince Yuri Dolgoruky of Suzdal and Vladimir invited one of his cousins to come and visit him there. It was an insignificant little place within his domain, a military outpost guarding the south-western approaches of his principality, and so it was to remain for the next 150 years, an outpost of little importance. This very remoteness, however, was one of the factors that played an important role in the emergence of Moscow eventually as the ruling principality of the land within the next historical period, and particularly during the time of the Tartar-Mongol tyranny, which lasted for nearly two and a half centuries (the whole of the Plantagenet period in English history, in fact).

Moscow's geographical situation was one of a combination of factors which enabled it to become the sovereign principality, in command of all the others, and eventually to lead them in the struggle to overpower the rule of the Great Khan. Because it was not on the great trade route used by the other merchant city-states, and because of the impenetrable forests which surrounded the city, the rival princes tended to ignore Moscow in their continual fights for supremacy. In the early eleventh century Grand Prince Yaroslav the Wise of Kiev instituted a system of succession whereby Kiev took precedence and was occupied by the most senior prince of the Rurikid family. The less senior princes governed in the other capitals, moving round by rota whenever a vacancy occurred, and this led to continual intrigue and violent dynastic strife. Because of its remoteness, Moscow was left out of this game of musical chairs and was able to ensure succession by primogeniture, which resulted in greater stability and authority. Moscow was also fortunate in being blessed with a series of able and strong ruling princes during the Tartar-Mongol suzerainty of the thirteenth and fourteenth centuries.

Daniel, the youngest son of Alexander Nevsky, was left undisturbed by his relations for many years, and eventually felt safe enough to proclaim himself Prince of Moscow in 1303. He was succeeded by his son, Ivan, who earned himself the label 'Kalita' (meaning purse or money bag), because of his skill with his exchequer. He pursued a clever, if shameful, policy of complete subjection to the Great Khan: he thoroughly ingratiated himself by frequent visits, carrying gifts and suffering all sorts of indignity, until he was granted the licence to collect and deliver from all the princes the tribute that had to be paid to keep the Tartar horde away. Ivan Kalita was able to exercise his power not only to collect up to double the necessary amount of tribute, but to expand his own domain and to threaten recalcitrant princes with a Tartar army as well as his own. Such force was too terrifying for any prince to think of defying it.

Ivan Kalita's successors continued his policy; with the support of the dignitaries of the Church, they soon established themselves as the supreme rulers of the Russian state and were confirmed in the position by the Great Khan. The Metropolitan Peter, head of the Church at Vladimir, where it had been since

---

Opposite: The Moscow Kremlin

the fall of Kiev in 1240, moved his see to Moscow in 1326, and when at the end of the century the famous ikon of the Virgin of Vladimir was brought to Moscow, supremacy was secure.

Under Great Prince Ivan III (1462–1505), Muscovy took its place among other states of the period in Europe, as an empire rising from the ruins of the feudal system. When Ivan III's first wife died, he was powerful enough to propose marriage to the niece of the last Byzantine emperor. She brought with her Italian architects, who transformed Moscow's ancient wooden walls and palisades into imposing castellated walls which survive to the present day, and built fine stone cathedrals with domes and fortifications able to withstand attacks from modern invaders.

Ivan III occasionally referred to himself as Tsar, a Russian version of Caesar, a title previously applied only to the Byzantine emperor or to the Great Khan himself. Ivan's son, Vassily III, and his grandson, Ivan IV, who came to the throne at the age of three, did the same, using the double-headed eagle emblem of the Byzantine rulers. When Ivan IV was finally crowned he was formally enthroned as Tsar of All Russia. In due course he acquired the name of 'Grozny', always translated as 'the Terrible', although 'awe-inspiring' would be more accurate.

When Great Prince Ivan III established Moscow's superi-ority it did not mean that he was safe from attack by his enemies. Russian history books give 1480 as the date of final liberation from the Tartar-Mongols, but onslaughts from the more distant khanates, in the Crimea and on the Volga, continued sporadically over the next 100 years and beyond. The powerful Lithuanians and Poles also repeatedly attempted to conquer Moscow's newly acquired domains, and from the thirteenth century onwards a protective necklace of fortified monasteries had grown up outside the city.

To commemorate the return to Russian hands of the fortress-city of Smolensk from Lithuania in 1524, Vassily III had added an important convent, known as Novodevichy (New Maidens) on the south-west approaches to the city. This is one of the most picturesque sights to be seen in Moscow (for the city has of course grown so that the convent is now well inside the city boundaries), and is, as one eminent historian describes it, 'an incomparable anthology of Moscow Baroque archi-tecture'. The main cathedral, dedicated to the Virgin of Smolensk (a famous ikon also kept in the cathedral until 1917), was built in 1525 and is an unadorned sixteenth-century structure with onion domes added a century later. Several churches and domestic buildings were added in the 1860s, with a multi-storeyed belfry which is often quoted as the pride of Moscow architecture.

Boris Godunov fled here with his sister Irina, widow of the last Tsar of the Rurikid dynasty, in 1598. On the steps of the cathedral he was acclaimed as the new Tsar by the crowd who had followed him there, while Irina remained in the convent as a nun. The building suffered severe damage from the invading Polish army in 1610. Peter the Great's forceful half-sister, Sophia, spent much effort and expense on rebuilding and embellishment, and was herself banished there after her unsuccessful plot to raise the Streltsy (Militia or Musketeers) against him in 1689. Peter had 300 of her co-conspirators hanged below the windows of her cell, and the hand of her chief supporter, Prince Khovansky, was nailed to her door. The whole story is thoroughly described in Rimsky-Korsakov's opera *Khovanshchina*. The Napoleonic soldiers occupied the convent in 1812 and had prepared to blow it up as they left, but the fuses were extinguished by brave nuns just in time to save it.

Another place which features in Moscow's early history is Kolomenskoe. Originally a village by that name, this was an estate of the Tsars much favoured for relaxation and entertainment. It was founded in the thirteenth century, and received an early mention in the chronicles in 1339. In the early sixteenth century Great Prince Vassily III and his son, Ivan IV, organized lavish hunts there and practised the favoured sport of all the early Tsars – falconry. Tsar Alexis, the second of the

Romanovs, was so enamoured of the place that he had an enormous timber palace built there in 1667, which took three years to complete. It was of great size and very picturesque, with more than 200 rooms, and surrounded by outhouses, entrance gates and churches.

One of the most spectacular churches in the Moscow region is that of the Virgin of Kazan at Kolomenskoe, erected in 1660 and embellished in 1880. With its striking blue domes with golden stars, it is all that remains today of the vast wooden palace, which had to be dismantled under the Empress Catherine II in the 1760s. Catherine did, however, have a wonderful scale model of it constructed so that we can now see what it looked like, and it is extremely impressive. An earlier church on the territory was consecrated in 1533, and built to celebrate the birth of Ivan, the future Ivan IV, the Terrible. Dedicated to the Feast of the Ascension, it is regarded as the finest example of a 'pyramid' or tent-shaped church in Russia. Tsar Alexis liked to spend much time here with his second wife, Natalia Naryshkin, and her son, Peter (to become Peter the Great) was born here in May 1672. Kolomenskoe also has a magnificent view from the high bank overlooking the Moskva river, a belfry from a vanished church of St George, and a water tower used also for falconry.

The Moscow Kremlin across the
Moskva river

Above: Red Square

Gatefold: The Novodevichy Convent

Above: The Hermitage, Kuskovo

Overleaf: The Kuskovo mansion

The Grotto, Kuskovo

The Chapel, Kuskovo

The Hermitage, Kuskovo

Above: Italian villa and waterfowl aviaries,
Kuskovo

Overleaf: Sukhanovo

Gatefold: Ostafievo

Above: Bridge, Marfino

Previous page: The Marfino mansion

Above: Abramtsevo

Abramtsevo

Abramtsevo

Above: The Ostankino mansion

Gatefold: The Church of the Resurrection
and falconry tower, Kolomenskoe

Above and overleaf: The Church of the Virgin
of Kazan, Kolomenskoe

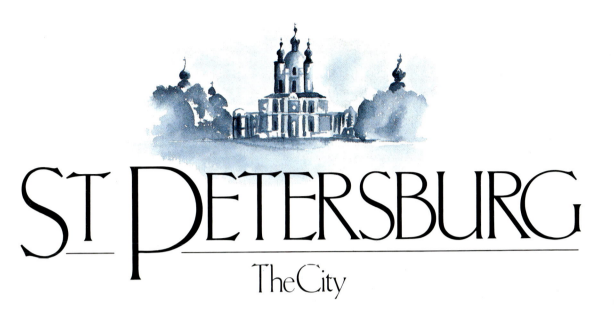

ST PETERSBURG

The City

Although I was born in Tiflis in the Caucasus and spent most of my life from the age of three in England, I have grown to love and admire St Petersburg as one does a poem one learns in one's childhood. Both my parents were born in the city, and they were married there. My elder brother was born at Tsarskoe Selo, and all through my early life at home I had heard about St Petersburg – from pictures on the walls, from lithographs, photographs and stories both serious and anecdotal – so that when I eventually got there, in the early sixties, I knew it intimately. I knew the names and position of the main streets, canals, bridges and buildings, and I soon found that I really loved the place and that it undoubtedly had a magic all its own.

There was the broad river Neva, with its rough surface, and the quietly flowing canals; the imposing Winter Palace; Palace Square, with the General Staff Arch and the Alexander Column in the centre; the fortress of Sts Peter and Paul; the Nevsky Prospect, most glamorous of main streets, conjuring up images of clattering hooves over squeaky snow as a carriage delivered some uniformed Guards officer to a secret assignation with a beautiful lady – all vivid dreams of a fertile, youthful imagination.

The city, and the spell it definitely casts, are the result of a harmonious combining of ingredients. The main artery is the river Neva, its roughness contrasting with the smoothness of the canals, whose names were as familiar to my young ears as the characters of fairy tales – Fontanka, Moika, Kriukov. Classical buildings, varying in style from early eighteenth century to late nineteenth, are of uniform height, with a few domes and steeples which rise proudly into an ever-changing sky – sometimes into rolling white clouds, other times into a misty wintry haze, and in summer and autumn, glorious sunsets. Of course, snow and ice and snowstorms are an integral ingredient of this northern Russian landscape.

St Petersburg was the capital of Peter the Great, and of the Golden Era of Catherine II; it was the inspiration of Russia's greatest poet, Alexander Pushkin, and the setting for his immortal dramas of *Eugene Onegin*, 'The Bronze Horseman' and *The Queen of Spades*. In this city Dostoievsky wrote *Crime and Punishment* and *The Brothers Karamazov*. St Petersburg was where Tchaikovsky had his greatest triumphs, and where all the greatest names in the Russian ballet world learned their first steps, at the Imperial (later Vaganova) Ballet School, and made their débuts on the stage of the Maryinsky (later Kirov) Theatre – Kshessinskaya, Pavlova, Karsavina, Spessivtseva, Fokine and Nijinsky, not of course forgetting Ulanova, Nureyev, Makarova and Baryshnikov. The Imperial Theatre was where Serge Diaghilev, the greatest impresario of all time (artistically, at least), was director in the years before he brought the glamour of the Russian Ballet to Western Europe. In St Petersburg, too, Fabergé master-minded most of his fabulous creations.

The White Nights of midsummer are visible throughout the northern part of Europe, but people from all over the world are particularly attracted to St Petersburg, where they can enjoy the special ambience and fascination of the city. At midnight you can read a newspaper in the street and the white colonnades of the palaces take on a disembodied quality as their ghostly reflections ripple on the quiet waters of the canals. The colour of the stucco of the buildings is unique. It was traditionally yellow, with the architectural features – pillars, window surrounds and cornices – in gleaming white. As taste and architects changed, additional colours appeared – brick red, green and pastel blue.

Peter the Great made a strategic choice for the site for his new capital, at the place where the broad river Neva flows into the gulf of Finland, the arm of the Baltic Sea which thrusts into Russian territory towards Lake Ladoga, but the terrain presented extraordinary difficulties for the building of a city. Tsar Peter was a determined as well as a powerful ruler,

Opposite: The Fortress of Sts Peter and Paul

however, and because it was impossible he announced that he was going to do it. In May 1703 he laid the foundation stone for the fortress of the Apostles Peter and Paul, and the city's first architect, Domenico Trezzini, an Italian from Switzerland, came from Denmark, where he had been working as a military engineer, and set the style for the first stone buildings of Peter's city.

All eighteenth-century monarchs employed prestigious foreign architects, and they brought with them staffs of craftsmen in painting, sculpture, wood-carving and stone-carving, glazing and ironwork. Peter was no exception in this respect, and foreigners began to stream into the new city of the Russian north – among the first, with Trezzini, were Fontana, Schädel and Schwertfeger. Peter even wrote personally to Sir Christopher Wren, inviting him to come to St Petersburg.

In 1715 the death of Louis XIV enabled Peter to entice Jean-Baptiste Le Blond to Russia, to lay out his Summer Palace and park with fountains at Peterhof, and to design the Summer Garden, the first of many parks within the city's precincts. The modest mansion in the Summer Garden was designed by Trezzini, who was also responsible for Peter's ministerial building – the Twelve Colleges – and the stone Cathedral inside the fortress of Sts Peter and Paul, which became a political prison and the burial place of Peter and subsequent sovereigns. In the space of twenty-two years, up to the time of Peter's death in 1725, were laid the foundations of a Baroque city which, by the end of the century, through the continuing efforts of his successors – mainly his daughter Elizabeth, followed by Catherine II – was to become the great Classical capital of the world.

It was during the reign of the Empress Anna that the greatest Baroque architect, Bartolomeo Rastrelli, began his phenomenal career, which reached its high point in the reign of Elizabeth. He arrived in Russia as a boy of sixteen with his father, Carlo, who was an eminent sculptor. His Baroque façades have undergone little change in the 200 years of their existence; in the city he was responsible for the Winter Palace, the Smolny Convent and Cathedral, and the palaces of the Counts Stroganov and Vorontsov. The latter was to house the famous Corps des Pages, where the sons of the nobility received a military-style education.

Two remarkable buildings from the earliest period of Peter the Great are Menshikov's Palace and Kikin's Mansion. Alexander Menshikov was Peter's closest friend and associate from their boyhood days. He was created a Prince and became the city's first Governor-General. Because of his unique relationship with the Tsar, Menshikov felt that he could get away with almost any extravagance, and in most cases this was true. From time to time, however, he went too far, and on those occasions Peter would physically attack him, thrashing him or boxing his ears. So it was with Menshikov's palace. Peter had

departed for the wars, leaving Menshikov in charge of the building of the Twelve Colleges and telling him that he could have a stretch of the Neva waterfront for his own palace. On his return, Peter found that the Colleges were built at right angles to the river and that Menshikov had appropriated a much wider frontage for himself. Having little interest in pomp and ceremony for himself, however, Peter used Menshikov's palace for his official receptions when he needed to impress a visiting notable. Peter's own modesty of taste is eloquently illustrated in Trezzini's Summer Palace, where he was quite content to live with his second wife, Catherine, who succeeded him as the Empress Catherine I.

With the accession in 1741 of Peter and Catherine's daughter Elizabeth, the talented Rastrelli began truly to dominate the architectural scene and the first phase of the city's dramatic growth to greatness was established. The waterfront embankments on each side of the Neva look like

eighteenth-century prints come to life. Rastrelli's Winter Palace, as befits the abode of the Autocrat, commands the whole panorama, and somehow manages to set the style of the glorious creations of the reign of Catherine II, the Great. This was the Golden Age of the city. Neo-classicism had appeared, and the new Empress's taste developed away from the earlier Baroque and its attendant Rococo decorations. Rastrelli was given a suitable reward and departed in none too good a mood for Warsaw. He died in 1771 in Courland, in the palace he had built there for the Empress Anna's favourite, the much-hated Biron.

The only architects who had worked for Elizabeth and who remained at the beginning of Catherine's reign were Vallin de la Mothe, appointed director of the Academy of Fine Arts (in the building designed by himself), and Kokorinov, who collaborated on the same building. Even the more mature Antonio Rinaldi, who had entered the service of her husband, the future Peter III, did not fulfil Catherine's new aspirations. She wrote to her artistic adviser abroad, the Baron Grimm, that she severely lacked suitable architects and designers for the Classical building programme she planned. She did, however, a few years later, give Rinaldi exclusively full rein for her private buildings at Oranienbaum.

During the 1770s two Russians emerged from the newly founded Academy of Arts and produced remarkable work: Yuri Veldten and Vassily Bazhenov. The former designed the beautiful wrought-iron railings in front of the Summer Garden, the Old or Large Hermitage front facing the Neva, and the remarkable little neo-Gothic church which commemorates the naval victory of Chesmé against the Turkish fleet in 1770. Bazhenov designed the Mikhailovsky Castle for Catherine's son, Paul, who had a paranoid terror of assassination; within forty days of moving in, he was murdered there in his own bedroom.

In the last years of the decade two foreigners arrived who were to contribute the real glories of St Petersburg Classicism.

The Scotsman Charles Cameron came in 1779, and the Italian Giacomo Quarenghi a year later. These are the men – to whom should be added another Russian, Ivan Starov, a fellow pupil of Bazhenov at the Academy – who established St Petersburg in the strictly Classical style. This lasted well into the 1830s, through the reigns of the Emperors Paul I and Alexander I, and into that of Nicholas I, culminating in the majestic work of Carlo Rossi. Although the name of Cameron is inextricably part of the essence of this epoch, none of his work is visible in the city itself, whereas that of Starov, Quarenghi and Rossi is very much in evidence all over the centre of St Petersburg. Rastrelli had gone, leaving his indelible mark, and there is a charming story which illustrates the veneration in which he was held. Quarenghi was charged with the task of building a school suitable for the pupils of the Smolny Convent, which had been found to be inappropriate for noble young ladies. On the way to his work at the Smolny Institute, he had to pass in front of Rastrelli's masterpiece, the Smolny Cathedral and Convent, and it is said that he daily used to raise his hat and incline his head

deferentially towards them, to show his respect for the old master. This was already in 1806–8, in the first decade of the reign of Catherine's grandson Alexander I. It is said that Quarenghi and Cameron were to Catherine's St Petersburg what Rastrelli was to Elizabeth's.

To complete the picture of Classical St Petersburg, a review of the contribution of Carlo Rossi is essential. During the summer a trip along the city's waterways is one of the best ways to see the main landmarks in the centre. The Neva's banks cover most of the Petrine period, and the three main canals provide splendid views of the Elizabethan and Catherine eras, as well as important aspects of later periods. The Kriukov canal is also worthwhile, giving a good and unusual sight of the beautiful golden domes and the separate belfry of the St Nicholas, or Sailors', Cathedral built by Rastrelli's Russian associate, Savva Chevakinsky. If the boat's captain can be persuaded to make a diversion to the Northern Nevka tributaries of the main river, one gets an extremely rewarding view of the Yelagin Palace and the Stone Island (Kamenniy Ostrov) Palace.

In the early 1800s, of course, these islands were country retreats. In 1817 the young Rossi, son of an Italian ballerina, and whose father some Russians suspect was the Emperor Paul, received his first commission from Alexander I, namely to adapt, both externally and internally, a private house which he had just bought there, into a suitable residence for his widowed Empress mother, Maria Feodorovna. Rossi succeeded so brilliantly in this difficult task that he then went on to become the foremost exponent of the Alexandrine Classical style, which is such a glory in all the most prominent parts of the city. Only Rossi could integrate so successfully the imposing sweep of the General Staff Arch, and the ministries on each side, with the imperious Winter Palace opposite. Only his genius could have successfully confronted Falconet's statue of the Bronze Horseman with the Senate-Synod building, to balance the stately and equally focal Admiralty of Zakharov.

As the grandson of the Grand Duke Michael, younger brother of Alexander I and Nicholas I, my mother's father was fortunate enough to inherit both the Stone Island Palace and the Michael Palace (now the Russian Museum), the latter perhaps Rossi's most successful residential creation. Here his fondness for comprehensive design and town planning is shown to the full. He designed the whole square, including the railings in front of the palace, and even the furniture inside. However, the most fitting monument to his talents has been the renaming of Theatre Street as Rossi Street. The perfect architectural proportions of the buildings behind the Alexandrine (now Pushkin) Theatre – also from his design – stand as a perpetual memorial to the Classical master of the incomparable St Petersburg.

Previous page: The Smolny Convent

Above: Mikhailovsky (Engineers') Castle

Gatefold: The Winter Palace and the Neva embankment

Above and overleaf: The river Neva

St Isaac's Cathedral and Senate buildings

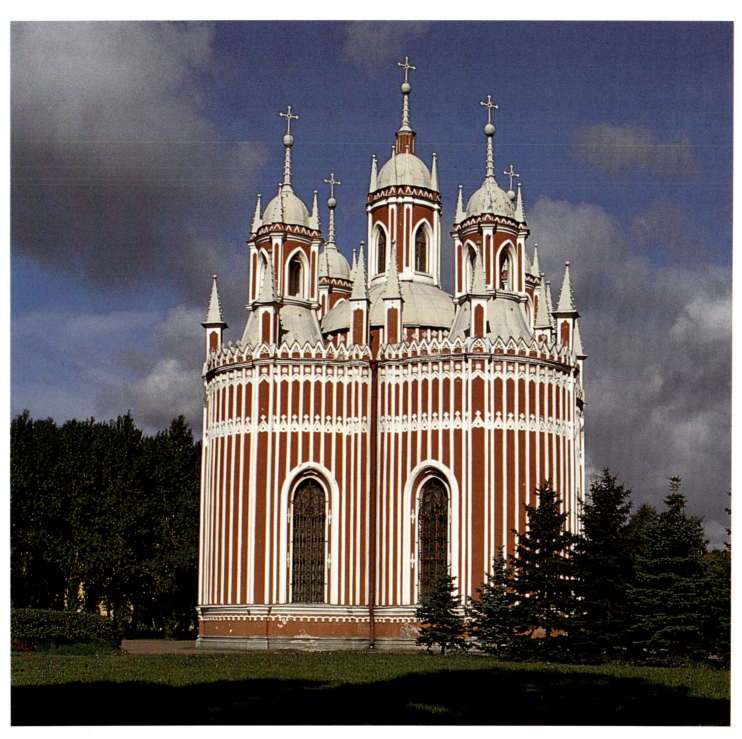

Chesme church

Above: The belfry of the St Nicholas
Cathedral (Sailors' Church)

Overleaf: Kikin's mansion

Previous page: The Michael Palace

Above: The Yelagin Palace

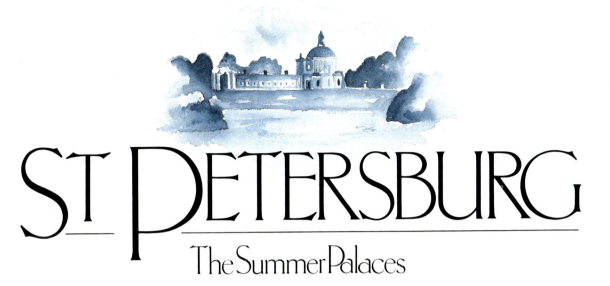

ST PETERSBURG

The Summer Palaces

Oranienbaum (Lomonosov)

The first summer palace was that of Alexander Menshikov on the southern shore of the gulf of Finland, although Peter the Great had already started work at Peterhof. Menshikov's Grand Palace at first consisted of a central block on a raised promontory overlooking the sea, but soon afterwards single-storey quadrant galleries were added on each side, leading to large pavilions with domed roofs. A canal was dug from the sea right up to the palace quay, in front of a formal garden. This canal was wide and deep enough to enable men-of-war to sail in to the ornamental harbour. The central block and each pavilion had on the roof a large prince's crown in wood. Today only the one in the centre remains, and has been carefully restored. The Western pavilion was a church; the other, the so-called Japanese pavilion, contained a hall used for receptions and balls.

The Grand Palace at Oranienbaum witnessed several dramatic events. Menshikov spent his last peaceful days there with his family before being summoned to Moscow, where he was to meet his downfall at the hands of the boy Tsar, Peter II. In 1718 the splendid palace was taken over by the Crown, and was completely neglected until 1737, when it was handed over to the Admiralty for use as a naval hospital. In 1743 the Empress Elizabeth, Peter the Great's daughter, presented it to her fifteen-year-old nephew, whom she had summoned from Holstein to be her heir apparent. Two years later he was to marry the girl who would eventually oust him from his throne to become Catherine II, the Great. She and her husband spent their summer months at Oranienbaum, and he spent most of his reign as Peter III there. It was at Oranienbaum that he signed the Instrument of Abdication in the presence of Catherine's favourite, Gregory Orlov, and two more of her emissaries, General Izmailov and Prince Galitzine.

It was also here that the young Catherine first met the Polish Prince Stanislaus Poniatowsky, devastatingly handsome and an elegant dancer, in the suite of the newly arrived British ambassador, Sir Charles Hanbury-Williams. The Polish Adonis received Catherine's ultimate favours, including finally the throne of Poland itself. From Catherine's youngest grandson, Michael, my mother's father (his grandson) inherited Oranienbaum, and my mother was born in the Grand Palace. My parents also lived there for a short period after they were married, and so it is particularly high in my affections.

Between 1748 and 1751 Rastrelli made some radical changes to the Grand Palace during rebuilding, as did others at various times, but the name most associated with Oranienbaum is that of Antonio Rinaldi. The then Grand Duke Peter, heir to the throne, asked Rinaldi to build him a small private villa, followed by a toy fortress of which only one of the entrance gates is visible today. In 1762, shortly after Catherine had completed her coup and usurped her husband's throne, she kept Rinaldi working there. Nowhere else has any architect in Russia reigned so supreme as Rinaldi did at Oranienbaum, building for Catherine a modest one-storey private palace, with seventeen rooms, which has recently been internationally acclaimed as an architectural masterpiece. It is called the Chinese Palace – although only three or four rooms are decorated in the Chinese Rococo style.

The most curious of Rinaldi's creations is the Switchback Pavilion (Katalnaya Gorka). This is an extravagant but beautiful folly which is the only part now remaining of a whole structure built for a day's amusement in the manner of the eighteenth century. A visiting Englishman, Archdeacon Coxe, described it in 1784 as 'the mountain of sledges'. It was the pavilion from which participants used to embark on a precipitate descent down an artificial slope known as a *montagne russe*, on a specially designed little cart on rails in summer, and on a sledge in winter. Inside the pavilion the guests relaxed or watched from the balustrades as others played. One of the rooms displayed porcelain groups specially modelled at Meissen, which were my grandfather's most treasured possessions. In the nineteenth century the structure became dangerous as the result of disuse and was dismantled, but the Folly itself remains a delight.

Peterhof

Since 1944 Peterhof has been known by its Russian name, Petrodvorets. Soon after founding the Fortress of Sts Peter and Paul in the city, Peter decided to build another, on the island of Kotlin in the approaches to the Gulf of Finland, and on his journeys to and fro he used to stop on the coast at a convenient promontory. Here he had a small house built in the Dutch style, which he named Mon Plaisir and which remained his favourite resort outside the city. Peter then planned a summer palace in the area of Mon Plaisir to emulate Versailles, with water and fountains as the main attraction. In the archives of the Hermitage are the sketches Peter is reputed to have made and which the architects used.

Peter's vision of a Russian Versailles was given impetus when Le Nôtre's talented pupil, Jean-Baptiste Le Blond, came to work for him in 1717. Peter had been impressed when he met Le Blond at Versailles, and immediately hired him to replace his chief architect, Schlüter, who had died a year after having taken over from Trezzini. Le Blond's stay in Russia was not particularly happy, but it was very productive. He arrived when Peter was away from home, and to begin with got off on the wrong foot with Menshikov. However, he drew plans for the layout of the new park at Peterhof, as well as exploiting the inspired location of the palace, using a very unusual sixty-foot-

high ridge running parallel to the seashore from which to overlook the cascade of fountains which are its dominant feature. Unfortunately Le Blond lasted only three years in Russia, and died of smallpox at the age of thirty-six.

While the Grand Palace was being built, Le Blond, in collaboration with Braunstein, who had been there from the beginning in 1713, and with Nicolo Michetti, a pupil of Fontana, designed and built two enchanting villa-like pavilions in the French manner, known as Marly and the Hermitage. Marly is a small building in front of a shallow lake, where gondolas used to provide entertainment for the guests and firework displays were regularly enjoyed. The Hermitage had a moat and drawbridges around it, and had an oval table, seating fourteen, which was winched up from the floor below so that the guests could eat their meal without the presence of servants. Unfortunately this mechanism no longer survives.

Peter took a great personal interest in the design and functioning of the fountains at Peterhof. The water came from Ropsha, some fifteen miles behind the Upper Park. The water from the river there is caught in lakes, then piped downhill to Peterhof; the fountains drain straight into the sea. Le Blond's original palace was only as wide as the width of the great cascade, and was a modest two-storey building with a central section and two wings. Rastrelli later enlarged the whole palace in the reign of Elizabeth, adding a third storey and widening the central section to double the size, although he took great care to preserve the original design. Rastrelli also added two pavilions at each end of the wings; one was a church, the other a heraldic pavilion topped by an eagle with three heads, only two of which are visible at any one time.

After Peter's death Peterhof was neglected for fifteen years, apart from one or two recorded visits by his widow, Catherine I, until his daughter Elizabeth renewed work on the Grand Palace. The Empress Anna is known, however, to have visited Mon Plaisir, and Catherine the Great spent much time there. It was from Peterhof that Catherine made her momentous departure on the night that her husband was due there from Oranienbaum to dine, and perhaps to carry out his threat to divorce her and send her to a convent, and it was while staying at Mon Plaisir, she wrote in her memoirs, that she first listened to the plans of the Orlov brothers to take Peter prisoner and proclaim her his successor.

The Grand Palace was never used by any sovereign except as a ceremonial site for great occasions or visiting dignitaries, although Mon Plaisir remained a favourite private retreat, as it had been for Peter the Great, who used it for transacting state business with specially invited guests and for his famous carousals. There is an interesting document, written in Peter's own hand, which lays down rules of behaviour for the guests at Mon Plaisir. Only those allocated a number for the bed they were to occupy were allowed to stay the night, and rule 4 said that you were not to lie on your bed in your boots or shoes.

In the Upper Park is an interesting fountain, which stands in the middle of a pond. Depicting Neptune with his three-pronged fork, it was made in the 1650s at Nüremberg and intended for the market-place there, but when it was delivered to the foundry for casting, the holes were discovered to be inadequate for the amount of water intended. It was not until 1799 that the Nüremberg Council sold it to the Emperor Paul for 66,000 gulden, and it came to Peterhof.

Tsarskoe Selo (Pushkin)

Tsarskoe Selo was renamed Pushkin in 1937, on the centenary of the poet's death. The original name is derived from the Finnish word *saari*, meaning 'high place', which became Tsarskoe. Selo means village. The ground is relatively higher than the surrounding plain, and the air is more pleasant than in the city. Peter's wife decided to build a modest stone house in this rural setting in 1718, during one of his frequent absences, and employed Braunstein, who was working at Peterhof and Kronstadt, to carry out her orders. Peter liked the place, but he infinitely preferred to be near water, near the sea, and took little notice of it. In 1728, after Catherine had died, the house was given to her daughter Elizabeth. Elizabeth was in a difficult position during the reigns of her nephew Peter II and her cousin Anna. It was not until 1740 that her dynastic claims were recognized, with the help of the powerful army element, and she was persuaded to make her coup and seize the throne. From 1741 onwards she was able to realize all her plans for Tsarskoe Selo, and create a splendid palace in the Imperial Baroque style where she could entertain on a grand scale.

Elizabeth made her first building alterations with the help of Kvassov. He was a talented young architect who had succeeded Zemtsov, who had died after only two years' work. Rastrelli was busy in the city, but he designed some pavilions in the park, of which the Grotto and the Hermitage are visible today. He also erected a switchback structure, the predecessor of the *montagne russe* at Oranienbaum which eighteenth-century visitors always remarked on so eloquently, but unfortunately no signs of it remain today.

By the time Rastrelli's genius was appreciated by the Empress, he was in a position to give full rein to his creative ability and build the majestic Catherine Palace for his sovereign's entertainment requirements, using a great deal of the Rococo design that Kvassov had been attempting. Elizabeth always kept the name of her mother as the original owner, and because the letter 'E' in Russian is the initial for both Yekaterina (Catherine) and Elizabeth, the monogram version covered both Empresses' names.

The other large palace at Tsarskoe Selo was built by Quarenghi on the orders of Catherine the Great, for her favourite grandson, Alexander, and is known as the Alexander Palace. Set in an English-style park adjoining that of the Catherine Palace, it has a lake in front of it and its Classical columns and restrained dignity contrast with the more flamboyant extravagance of its neighbour. The last Emperor, Nicholas II, and his family used to spend the majority of their time at the Alexander Palace, and it was there that they were kept under house arrest by the Provisional Government after the Tsar's abdication in 1917, before being dispatched to Tobolsk in Siberia prior to their murder.

Russia's favourite poet, Alexander Pushkin, was educated from 1811 onwards at the Imperial Lyceum, a school built on to the chapel end of the Catherine Palace for future administrators. Pushkin was one of the first batch of these very exclusive pupils, and he never lost his love of the parks and ambience of Tsarskoe Selo. He knew every inch of the park, its statues, its monuments and lakes, and wrote many endearing poems on its themes.

Catherine the Great enjoyed the place and used it to the full, and Charles Cameron was most successful here on her behalf. He added a beautiful and magnificent covered walk at right angles to the western end of the great palace, which so delighted the Empress that she had it named the Cameron Gallery; and when she became older and heavy, he built a ramp at one end – a *pente douce* – up which she could be wheeled to reach the gallery without having to use her invalid legs. The word entered the Russian language: *pandus* means a slope of this sort. The Cameron Gallery contained rows of black marble busts of Greek philosophers and Roman emperors, to which Catherine added one of Charles James Fox because he was the opponent of William Pitt, Russia's adversary. The gallery adjoined Cameron's Agate Pavilion, built

for the Empress in 1784. It contained hot and cold baths, which Catherine could reach direct from her private apartments.

In the park were many pavilions and monuments, including one to Catherine's young lover, Alexander Lanskoy, whose death of diphtheria at the age of twenty-six had distressed her very much. Cameron also built a pyramid to contain the graves of her Italian greyhounds. Three of them are buried there: Sir Tom Anderson, his wife Duchesse, and Zemir.

Pavlovsk

Catherine the Great was so overjoyed at the birth of her first grandson, Alexander, in 1777, that she gave her son Paul and his wife, Maria Feodorovna, a present of about 1,500 acres of rich hunting grounds just two and a half miles away from Tsarskoe Selo. Cameron was instructed to give his services to Paul and Maria at Pavlovsk. Catherine had developed a passion for landscape gardening, as all her palaces bear witness. In the early 1770s she had recruited the services of John Busch, a Hanoverian who had a well-known nursery garden in Hackney. Busch came to St Petersburg, where he trained many artists and also inspired most of the architects who were working for Catherine. Most of his designs are in Gatchina and Tsarskoe Selo.

Cameron's first work at Pavlovsk was to design and arrange some pavilions and rustic cottages for Paul and Maria Feodorovna. The cottages were called Paullust (Paul's joy) and Marienthal (Maria's valley) and were built on the site of two timber hunting lodges known as 'Krik' and 'Krak'. After laying out large areas of the park, he was commissioned to design a palace in stone suitable to be the official summer residence of the heir to the throne. In 1782, soon after Cameron had started work, the Grand Duke Paul took his wife off on a tour of Europe, but before he left he brought in his own favourite architect, Vincenzo Brenna, to help Cameron with the palace

and the park project. Although Brenna and Cameron spent most of the time squabbling, the results are surprisingly happy. Paul and Maria, travelling as 'Le Comte and la Comtesse du Nord', spent a month in Paris and sent home a great number of artefacts to Pavlovsk.

Cameron's earliest masterpieces at Pavlovsk are the Temple of Friendship, the first instance of the Greek Doric style in Russia, and the Apollo Colonnade, on the bank across the Slavyanka river, opposite the palace. He took full advantage of the landscape features, choosing a commanding position on top of a steep bank overlooking the Slavyanka, and designed a building strongly reminiscent of an English country house of an earlier decade. The upper park, in front of the palace, had a formal French or Italian appearance, with a triple lime avenue facing the entrance, whereas the lower park along the river valley was much more in the English style. The façades of the palace, both front and back, are decorated with four pairs of columns on the first floor, giving an impression of Classical austerity as well as elegance, and making wonderful reflections in the river below. The pairs of white columns contrast pleasantly with the pale yellow of the background walls, and the whole is surmounted by a flat cupola held on a ring of small pillars.

Either because everything that his mother did or liked was anathema to Paul, or because he felt further away from her there, Paul took to making his home more at Gatchina, which he was given as soon as its original owner, Gregory Orlov, died in 1783. However, Maria Feodorovna loved and cherished Pavlovsk as her particular favourite and during the years of her widowhood – she lived until 1828 – she continually embellished the palace, its décor, its furnishings, as well as the park and landscape. Brought up in the château of Montbéliard, then an apanage of the Duchy of Württemberg, she had impeccable taste and a thorough artistic education, and Pavlovsk benefited from this in the five decades it took to complete it. Thanks to Maria Feodorovna, and in spite of a great number of artists having contributed, the complex of palace and park is a masterpiece of harmonious beauty.

In 1796 Paul became Emperor Paul I, and Pavlovsk became an official summer residence of the monarch. Paul had by now become absorbed with Gatchina, where Brenna had taken over the reconstruction of Gregory Orlov's castle-like palace. As Emperor, Paul felt free at last to dismiss Charles Cameron, his mother's favourite architect, and appoint Brenna at Pavlovsk as well as at Gatchina, but his freedom was short-lived. Paul was strangled on 24 March 1801, after moving into his supposedly impregnable Mikhailovsky Castle only forty days before. Incidentally, because of Paul's paranoid fear of assassination, Brenna had been largely responsible for the work of converting Bazhenov's designs for the castle into a secure stronghold.

Cameron was reinstated by Alexander I and returned to

fresh glories in the park at Pavlovsk. He married Catherine, daughter of the landscape maestro John Busch, and designed the Three Graces Pavilion at Pavlovsk for the Empress Mother Maria Feodorovna. In 1803, however, a serious fire destroyed much of the palace, and Andrei Voronikhin was invited to become chief architect in charge of a rapid restoration. This handsome young man, who was the illegitimate son of Count Stroganov and had been brought up with the Count's son as one of the family, had recently returned from a training visit to Europe. Even Brenna found favour in the sight of Maria Feodorovna. Giacomo Quarenghi also joined the band of those working at Pavlovsk, and the whole place hardly had a day's rest from builders and improvers until the Empress Mother's death in the third year of the reign of her third son, Nicholas I.

Brenna, with the help of Quarenghi, Voronikhin and later Rossi, enlarged the palace by adding semi-circular wings, while preserving Cameron's central classical building. After the fire, it was quickly restored to its former splendour with the invaluable help of a very detailed inventory compiled by Maria Feodorovna, listing each item and its position in each room. This inventory again came into its own when the Soviet restorers performed the monumental task of reconstruction and complete restoration after the Palace's devastation by the Wehrmacht during the terrible 900-day siege of Leningrad in 1941–4. The Nazi occupiers also felled thousands of trees in the park, which had to be replanted to recreate the Circles and Sylvia designs of Cameron and Brenna, the paths of Pietro Gonzago, and many bridges over the Slavyanka river, such as the Centaur bridge near the Cold Bath building, both by Cameron. His Apollo Colonnade was severely damaged by a storm in 1817, and Maria Feodorovna, in an inspired decision, left it half-ruined, as it remains today.

Finally, Russia's very first railway station was built at Pavlovsk; it incorporated a concert hall, which became a popular feature in the second half of the nineteenth century. Like all subsequent railway stations across Russia it was called Vokzal – Vauxhall – after the one in London. Johann Strauss, king of the waltz, came to conduct there for several seasons, and Berlioz also performed there.

Gatchina

Gatchina is a medieval-style castle lying about twenty miles south-west of St Petersburg. It was built in 1762 by Antonio Rinaldi, on the instructions of Catherine II, and presented to Gregory Orlov as a reward for the decisive role he had played in securing her the throne of her husband, Peter III. Between 1766 and 1781 Rinaldi also laid out the first landscape park in Russia, which was the forerunner of those at Tsarskoe Selo and Pavlovsk, and no doubt the arrival of John Busch from England added momentum to the landscaping activities which the new

Empress was so keen on. It seems somewhat surprising that Paul I should have taken so eagerly to Gatchina, seeing that it had been the summer palace of his mother's lover, whom he so hated, but he became passionately interested in his new residence after receiving it from his mother after Orlov's death in 1783. No doubt its beautiful setting, in a pattern of islands and lakes connected by stone bridges, together with the greater distance from his mother's residence at Tsarskoe Selo, attracted him. Needless to say, he soon had Vincenzo Brenna working at Gatchina, and the architect proceeded to make radical alterations to Rinaldi's creation, making it look even more like a medieval castle. Here Paul could indulge his favourite pastime – drilling his soldiers. In front of the palace is a vast parade ground, with a statue by Vitali of Paul on a pedestal, a second version of which is in front of the Pavlovsk palace.

Among the many attractions of Gatchina's park is a pavilion built of silver birch logs, which Maria Feodorovna had made as a surprise for her husband. The design is attributed to Nicholas Lvov, who also designed a priory on the banks of one of the many lakes, a reminder of Paul's proud appointment as Head of the Maltese Order of the Knights of St John of Jerusalem.

The Cottage

At one end of Alexandria Park, nearest to the city and to Strelna, Peter the Great's other seaside resort before reaching Peterhof, is a relatively modest yellow house standing on a natural terrace overlooking the Gulf of Finland. It is named the Cottage, and was built in the neo-Gothic style in 1826–9 by a Scottish architect called Adam Menelaws for Nicholas I, who gave it to his wife, Alexandra Feodorovna. The Empress, a shy and retiring Prussian princess, disliked the pomp and ceremony of the court and preferred to spend her time in seclusion, surrounded by her family. She had been born Charlotte of Prussia, but was rechristened Alexandra when she embraced Russian Orthodoxy. All the foreign princesses who married into the Russian Imperial family had to go through this change of name when adopting Orthodoxy, unless they happened to have already been christened with the name of a saint in the Orthodox calendar.

At the outbreak of the Second World War, as many valuables as possible from the outlying palaces of St Petersburg were evacuated or removed and buried. Between 1941 and 1944 the German army occupied all the palaces, with the sole exception of Oranienbaum; all were badly damaged, and they have been painstakingly and magnificently restored – a process which still continues. Oranienbaum, the only genuine and original palace from the eighteenth century, is unique in this respect, and for this reason is the subject of special pride to its curators.

Gatefold: Tsarskoe Selo (Pushkin), Catherine
Palace

Above: Peter the Great

Above: The Grand Palace, Petrodvorets
(Peterhof)

Overleaf: Marly, Petrodvorets

Above: Mon Plaisir, Petrodvorets

Above: Gatchina

Gatefold: Pavlovsk

Above: Pavlovsk

Overleaf: The park, Pavlovsk

Above: Oranienbaum

Previous page and above: Katalnaya Gorka
(Switchback Pavilion), Oranienbaum

Acknowledgements

While working on our first production – *The Treasure Houses of England* – in 1988, it became our ambition to photograph and produce a book showing the grandeur of the architecture of old Russia and its splendid landscape settings. *Imperial Splendour* is the result of this ambition, a photographic record of some of that country's finest buildings, compiled for the pleasure of future generations from both east and west.

Producing this book has been an assignment of sheer delight: being allowed to tour and photograph Russia as we pleased, which also gave us an insight into a culture totally different from our own, and meeting and being made welcome by its people at all levels, has been a rare privilege.

The photography, however, is only a part of producing a publication such as this. The photographs have to be catalogued, shortlisted and a final selection made for inclusion in the book; the format of the book has to be designed, and the finished artwork produced for the printer. The design task was made easier for us by the able assistance of our own Julie Wigg, who put in more hard work than could have been expected of her and who also produced the wonderful wash illustrations for the book.

During our initial research for the book we met Dr Dominic Lieven, of the London School of Economics. He introduced us to Prince George Galitzine, who not only wrote the text for the book but also acted as adviser to us on which areas of Russia we should photograph and arranged our travel schedule.

We would also like to thank all the other people involved to whom we owe our gratitude: Eleo Gordon, Joy Harrison, Janice Beesley, Felicity Hill, Anne Lee and Christopher Brown. A special mention must go to our drivers and guides, who willingly assisted us without complaint at all times of the day, from the crack of dawn until sunset and during the perishing cold of the Russian winter.

It is now our wish to return to this beautiful country and photograph for a second volume, as there is far more material than we could possibly use in just one book. We hope this wish will be granted.

Earl Beesley
Garry Gibbons